Electric Pressure Cooker

INSTANT POT

Cookbook

365 Easy and Delicious Recipes for your Electric Pressure Cooker Instant Pot

by Samanta Klein

Contents

Contents

Beef, Lamb and Pork.. 115

Stews and Chilies 141

Pasta 173

Fish and Seafood...193

Desserts 225

Chef's Selection of Recipes 244

Introduction

Just because you don't know how to cook more than steamed veggies and steak in your Instant Pot, it doesn't mean that this appliance is a waste of money.

Dive into the depths of this book and find out that the possibilities with Instant Pot cooking are pretty endless.

From yummy breakfasts, to meat, seafood, and veggies, to pasta, rice, risotto, and stocks, sauces, and dessert. Whatever your taste buds are craving, you can find it in this book. You can literary cook anything in the Instant Pot—from eggs to cakes—and this book will show you how.

And the best part? Inside you will find a bonus chapter that will reward you with some fancy-looking and restaurant-like holiday and party recipes that will make you the host of the year.

What are you waiting for? Your yummy dinner is just a click of the button away.

Cooking with the Instant Pot

There are several cooking mode buttons on the Instant Pot. Understanding them is important for effortless cooking with the Instant Pot.

MANUAL – Manual is the most used cooking mode, and allows you to set your own cooking time.

+ AND - – Use these to increase or decrease the cooking time.

ADJUST – Use this to adjust the settings to their in-built default mode.

PRESSURE – Switch between LOW and HIGH pressure.

KEEP WARM/CANCEL – Use this to either cancel cooking, or use your Instant Pot as a warmer to keep your meal warm until ready to serve.

SLOW COOK – You can use your Instant Pot as a slow cooker.

STEAM – Use to steam veggies. The default setting is10 minutes.

YOGURT – Use this to make yogurt. You can also pasteurize milk on the less setting, or even make porridges on the more setting.

RICE – Use this to cook rice. This setting automatically cooks on LOW pressure, but you can change that if you like.

MEAT/STEW – Default cooking time is 35 minutes. Use this setting for cooking meat and making stews.

BEAN/CHILI – Default setting is 30 minutes. Use this setting for cooking bean dishes and chilies.

POULTRY – Default setting is 15 minutes. Use this setting for cooking poultry.

SOUP – Default setting is 30 minutes.

MULTIGRAIN – Great for preparing grains. Default setting is for 40 minutes.

PORRIDGE – If you love porridges you will be pleased to know that you can know make them with a convenient click of a button.

The Pressure

Some people find releasing the pressure to be overwhelming. Will it spill or not? However, there is nothing to worry about when you know which method to use when.

Quick Pressure Release – This means quickly letting all of the pressure and steam release from the Instant Pot. That is good when cooking veggies, seafood, or even meat. However, you need to be careful, and note that if your Instant Pot is full, releasing the pressure quickly will most likely result in spillage.

Natural Pressure Release – This is the solution method for soups, foamy foods, or for those meals that are larger in volume.

Tips Instant Pot

Still overwhelmed with your new appliance? Don't worry! These tips will get you started in a jiffy:

- Do not overfill the Instant Pot. Crowding the pot may result in clogging the valve and increasing the pressure. Do not fill the Instant Pot more than 2/3 full. If cooking something that may increase in size during as it cooks, fill the Instant Pot only halfway.

- Never force open the lid. Always make sure that the pressure has been fully released before opening the lid, to avoid any injuries.

- Don't use more liquid than necessary, since it will only dilute flavor. A rule of a thumb is to use 1½ cups of water.

- Always leave the meat on room temperature for at least half an hour before cooking (for all kind of meats).

- When using frozen foods, just increase the cooking time a bit.

- Make it a habit to check the sealing ring before cooking. They have the tendency to deform after a certain time period. Replace it after 18 months.

The Benefits

If you have ever listened to some late-night infomercials about kitchen appliances and cooking gadgets, then you are probably familiar with the whole throw-away-everything-because-this-is-the-only-appliance-you-will-ever-need thing. Not to sound cliché, but the Instant Pot is the perfect definition of that.

Probably the biggest advantage of this cooking appliance is that you will get 7 different appliances for the price of one, packed in one fancy-looking pot:

1. Electric pressure cooker
2. Sauté pan
3. Rice cooker
4. Slow cooker
5. Steamer
6. Warmer
7. Yogurt maker

And if that isn't worth the money, I don't know what is. Those who will especially appreciate the Instant Pot are those with tiny kitchens with limited space.

But that is not the only reason you should switch to Instant Pot cooking; buying the Instant Pot will bring you other benefits, too:

- **Time and energy saving.** The Instant Pot uses 70% less energy than other cooking methods. That will, obviously, save you money on your electrical bill. But that is not the only thing it saves. The Instant Pot also cooks food 70% faster than other appliances, which makes cooking pretty convenient for busy people.

- **Nutrient preservation.** If you pay attention to your vitamin and mineral intake then you will be thrilled to know that food cooked in the Instant Pot – unlike steaming veggies on the stove – preserves all of its nutrients, thanks to the even, pressure cooking.

- **No harmful substances** – When you cook with pressure, the food is always cooked at the temperature that is actually above the point of boiling water. That means that any harmful substances that may have been in the uncooked food are killed during the cooking process.

Breakfast

Bacon and Paprika Scrambled Eggs

(Prep + Cook Time: 15 minutes / Servings: 4)

Nutritional Info per Serving:

Calories 290, Protein 16, Carbs 4.5, Fat 23.4

Ingredients:

1 tsp. basil, chopped
7 eggs
1 tbsp. chopped cilantro
4 oz. bacon, chopped

1 tsp. paprika
1 tsp. salt
Pinch of black pepper

Directions:

1. Whisk together the eggs, spices, cilantro, and basil, in a bowl. Select SAUTÉ.
2. Place the bacon in the Instant Pot and sauté for 3 minutes.
3. Add the egg mixture and cook for 5 more minutes.
4. Scramble the eggs with a wooden spoon and cook for 3 more minutes.

Sausage and Cheddar Frittata

(Prep + Cook Time: 45 minutes / Servings: 4)

Nutritional Info per Serving:

Calories 282, Protein 16, Carbs 1, Fat 12

Ingredients:

½ cup ground breakfast sausage
2 tbsp. sour cream
¼ cup grated cheddar cheese

4 eggs
1 ½ cups water
Salt and pepper, to taste

Directions:

1. Pour the water into the Instant Pot and lower the rack.
2. Spray a soufflé dish with cooking spray.
3. Whisk together the eggs, sour cream, and some salt and pepper.
4. Stir in the sausage and cheddar cheese.
5. Pour the mixture into the soufflé dish, and cover with aluminum foil.
6. Place on the rack, close the lid, and select MANUAL.
7. Cook for 17 minutes on LOW.
8. Do a quick pressure release.
9. Serve and enjoy!

Creamy Oatmeal with Peaches

(Prep + Cook Time: 20 minutes / Servings: 4)

Nutritional Info per Serving:

Calories 200, Protein 6, Carbs 31, Fat 3

Ingredients:

1 peach, chopped
4 cups water
2 cups rolled oats

1 tsp. vanilla
2 tbsp. flax meal
1 tbsp. maple syrup

Directions:

1. Place everything in your Instant Pot. Stir to combine well.
2. Close the lid, select MANUAL, and cook on HIGH for 3 minutes.
3. Allow pressure to release naturally, about 10 minutes.
4. Serve and enjoy!

Thyme-Flavored Tomato and Spinach Eggs

(Prep + Cook Time: 35 minutes / Servings: 6)

Nutritional Info per Serving:

Calories 178, Protein 15.3, Carbs 5, Fat 11

Ingredients:

½ cup milk
1½ cups water
12 eggs
1 tsp. dried thyme
¼ cup grated Parmesan cheese
3 large scallions, sliced

1 cup tomato, chopped
½ tsp. salt
3 cups baby spinach
4 tomato slices
¼ tsp. black pepper

Directions:

1. Pour the water into the Instant Pot.
2. Whisk the eggs along with the milk, salt, thyme, and pepper, in a bowl.
3. Grease a baking dish with cooking spray, and combine the chopped tomatoes and spinach in it.
4. Pour the eggs over.
5. Sprinkle the scallions over eggs, and top with the tomato slices.
6. Sprinkle with Parmesan cheese.
7. Place the dish inside the Instant Pot, and close the lid.
8. Select MANUAL, and cook on HIGH for 20 minutes.
9. Allow pressure to release naturally.
10. Serve and enjoy!

Pomegranate Porridge

(Prep + Cook Time: 5 minutes / Servings: 4)

Nutritional Info per Serving:

Calories 400, Protein 14, Carbs 70, Fat 6

Ingredients:

2 cups oats

1 ½ cups pomegranate juice

1 ½ cups water

2 tbsp. pomegranate molasses

Pinch of sea salt

Directions:

1. Place the water, oats, salt, and juice in your Instant Pot.
2. Stir to combine and close the lid.
3. Select MANUAL, and cook for 3-½ minutes on HIGH.
4. Do a quick pressure release.
5. Stir in the pomegranate molasses
6. Serve and enjoy!

Cheesy Egg Cups with Spinach

(Prep + Cook Time: 15 minutes / Servings: 6)

Nutritional Info per Serving:

Calories 114, Protein 11, Carbs 2, Fat 7

Ingredients:

½ tsp. salt

½ cup shredded mozzarella cheese

6 eggs

1 tsp. black pepper

1 cup chopped spinach, divided

1 cup water1 tomato, chopped

¼ cup crumbled feta cheese

Directions:

1. Pour the water into your Instant Pot. Lower the trivet.
2. Divide the spinach between silicone ramekins.
3. Whisk together the eggs, salt, and pepper, in a bowl.
4. Stir in the remaining ingredients. Divide that mixture between the ramekins.
5. Place in the Instant Pot.
6. Select MANUAL, and cook on HIGH for 8 minutes.
7. Do a quick pressure release.

Bacon and Cheddar Egg Muffins

(Prep + Cook Time: 20 minutes / Servings: 4)

Nutritional Info per Serving:

Calories 70, Protein 4.6, Carbs 1.5, Fat 2.4

Ingredients:

1½ cups water

4 bacon slices, cooked and crumbled, divided

¼ tsp. lemon pepper seasoning

4 eggs

1 scallion, chopped and divided

4 tbsp. shredded cheddar cheese, divided

A pinch of salt

Directions:

1. In a bowl, whisk together the eggs, lemon pepper, and salt.
2. Divide the cheese onion and bacon, between 4 silicon muffin cups.
3. Pour the egg mixture over.
4. Pour the water into your Instant Pot and arrange the muffin cups on the rack.
5. Close the lid, select MANUAL, and cook on HIGH for 10 minutes.
6. Do a quick pressure release.
7. Serve and enjoy!

Egg and Rice Breakfast Porridge

(Prep + Cook Time: 45 minutes / Servings: 4)

Nutritional Info per Serving:

Calories 214, Protein 10, Carbs 24, Fat 2

Ingredients:

½ cup white rice, rinsed and drained
2 cups chicken broth
4 eggs
½ tsp. salt
1 tbsp. sugar

2 cups water
4 scallions, chopped
2 tsp. soy sauce
1 tbsp. olive oil
Pinch of black pepper

Directions:

1. Combine the broth, water, salt, sugar, and rice, in your Instant Pot.
2. Select PORRIDGE, and cook for 30 minutes on HIGH.
3. Do a quick pressure release, and set aside in a separate bowl.
4. Turn the SAUTÉ mode on, and heat the olive oil.
5. Add eggs, soy sauce, scallions, and pepper, and stir with a wooden spoon.
6. Stir in the rice and cook for 2 minutes, or until the porridge thickens.

Bacon and Cheese Hash Brown Breakfast

(Prep + Cook Time: 10 minutes / Servings: 4)

Nutritional Info per Serving:

Calories 164, Protein 12, Carbs 7, Fat 11

Ingredients:

4 eggs
½ tsp. salt and black pepper
1 cup frozen hash browns

3 bacon slices, chopped
¼ cup milk
½ cup grated cheddar cheese

Directions:

1. Turn Instant Pot to SAUTÉ, and cook the bacon until crispy, about 2 minutes.
2. Add the hash browns, and cook for 2 more minutes.
3. Whisk the eggs, milk, salt, pepper, and cheese, in a bowl.
4. Pour this mixture over the bacon and hash browns, and close the lid.
5. Select MANUAL, and cook for 5 minutes.
6. Do a quick pressure release.

Three Meat Quiche

(Prep + Cook Time: 45 minutes / Servings: 4)

Nutritional Info per Serving:

Calories 419, Protein 29, Carbs 4.1, Fat 32

Ingredients:

1½ cups water
6 eggs
4 bacon slices, cooked and crumbled
½ cup milk
¼ tsp. salt½ cup diced ham

1 cup cooked ground sausage
Pinch of black pepper
1 cup grated cheddar cheese
2 scallions, chopped

Directions:

1. Pour the water into your Instant Pot.
2. Whisk the eggs along with the salt, pepper, and milk, in a bowl.
3. In a 1-quart baking dish, add the bacon, sausage, ham, and mix to combine.
4. Pour the eggs over, and stir to combine again.
5. Sprinkle with green onions and cheese.
6. Cover with foil and place in the Instant Pot.
7. Select MANUAL, and cook on HIGH for 30 minutes.
8. Do a quick pressure release.

Coconut and Chia Pudding

(Prep + Cook Time: 45 minutes / Servings: 4)

Nutritional Info per Serving:

Calories 130, Protein 14, Carbs 2, Fat 12

Ingredients:

½ cup chia seeds

4 tsp. sugar

¼ cup chopped almonds

¼ cup shredded coconut

2 cups almond milk

Directions:

1. Place all of the ingredients into your Instant Pot.

2. Stir to combine well and close the lid. Select MANUAL, and cook on HIGH for 3 minutes. Do a quick pressure release.

Italian Sausage and Peppers

(Prep + Cook Time: 45 minutes / Servings: 4)

Nutritional Info per Serving:

Calories 400, Protein 23, Carbs 8, Fat 30

Ingredients:

1 tbsp. dried basil

15 oz. tomato sauce

28 oz. canned diced tomatoes

4 green bell peppers, cut into strips

8 Italian sausages

1 cup water

1 tbsp. Italian seasoning

2 tsp. minced garlic

Directions:

1. Pour the water into your Instant Pot. In a baking dish, place all of the ingredients. Stir to combine. Place the dish in the Instant Pot, and close the lid.

2. Select MANUAL, and cook on HIGH for 25 minutes. Do a quick pressure release.

Simple Steel Cut Oats

(Prep + Cook Time: 10 minutes / Servings: 4)

Nutritional Info per Serving:

Calories 155, Protein 4, Carbs 28, Fat 2

Ingredients:

3 cups water, divided
1 cup steel cut oats

1 cup milk, warm
2 tsp. sugar

Directions:

1. Pour 1 cup of water in your Instant Pot.
2. In a heatproof bowl, combine the oats and 2 cups of water.
3. Place the bowl on the trivet.
4. Close the lid, select MANUAL, and cook on HIGH for 6 minutes.
5. Release the pressure quickly.
6. Stir in the milk and the sugar.
7. Serve and enjoy!

Vanilla French Toast

(Prep + Cook Time: 35 minutes / Servings: 4)

Nutritional Info per Serving:

Calories 183, Protein 8, Carbs 21, Fat 3

Ingredients:

1 ½ cups water
3 large eggs

3 cups cubed cinnamon swirl bread
1 tsp. butter

1 tsp. vanilla extract

2 tbsp. maple syrup

1 cup whole milk

1 tsp. sugar

Directions:

1. Pour the water into your Instant Pot. Lower the rack.
2. Grease a baking pan with the butter.
3. In a bowl, whisk the eggs along with the milk, sugar, maple syrup, vanilla extract, and salt.
4. Arrange the bread cubes in the pan, and pour the egg mixture over.
5. Place the baking dish on the rack, and close the Instant Pot.
6. Select MANUAL, and cook on HIGH for 15 minutes.
7. Release the pressure quickly.

Chili Poached Eggs with Tomatoes

(Prep + Cook Time: 15 minutes / Servings: 4)

Nutritional Info per Serving:

Calories 194, Protein 10, Carbs 8.45, Fat 13.5

Ingredients:

½ tsp. paprika

1 tsp. chili powder

3 tomatoes, chopped

1 small red onion, chopped

1 tsp. salt

1 tbsp. chopped fill

1½ cup water

1 tbsp. olive oil

Directions:

1. Pour the water into the Instant Pot and lower the rack.
2. Grease 4 ramekins with the olive oil.
3. Crack the eggs into the ramekins and whisk them slightly.
4. In a bowl, combine the rest of the ingredients and divide this mixture between the ramekins.

5. Place the ramekins on the rack and close the lid.
6. Select STEAM, and cook for 5 minutes.

Banana Bread Oatmeal

(Prep + Cook Time: 25 minutes / Servings: 4)

Nutritional Info per Serving:

Calories 370, Protein 10, Carbs 50, Fat 12

Ingredients:

½ cup walnuts, chopped
3-⅓ cups water
2 cups oatmeal
1 tsp. vanilla

2 bananas, mashed
¼ cup honey
Pinch of salt

Directions:

1. Place all of the ingredients into the Instant Pot.
2. Stir to combine well.
3. Close the lid, select PORRIDGE.
4. Cook for 10 minutes.
5. Allow pressure to release naturally.
6. Serve and enjoy!

Oats and Apricots

(Prep + Cook Time: 10 minutes / Servings: 4)

Nutritional Info per Serving:

Calories 236, Protein 4.5, Carbs 22, Fat 4.1

Ingredients:

1 cup steel cut oats

1 cup coconut milk

2 apricots, diced
½ tsp. vanilla extract

Directions:

1. Place all of the ingredients into your Instant Pot.
2. Close the lid, select MANUAL, and cook on HIGH for 3 minutes.
3. Allow pressure to release naturally, for about 10 minutes.
4. Serve and enjoy!

Almond and Rolled Oats

(Prep + Cook Time: 10 minutes / Servings: 4)

Nutritional Info per Serving:

Calories 288, Protein 5, Carbs 39, Fat 4.5

Ingredients:

2 cups almond milk
½ cup chopped almonds
1 cup rolled oats
¼ cup sugar

1 tbsp. coconut oil
2 cups chopped pears
Pinch of cinnamon
Pinch of salt

Directions:

1. Set your Instant Pot to SAUTÉ.
2. Add the coconut oil and cook until melted.
3. Stir in all of the remaining ingredients.
4. Close the lid, select MANUAL, and cook on HIGH for 6 minutes.
5. Allow pressure to release naturally.
6. Serve and enjoy!

Easy Chicken Soup
with Carrots and Potatoes

(Prep + Cook Time: 50 minutes / Servings: 4)

Nutritional Info per Serving:

Calories 72, Protein 9, Carbs 7, Fat 8

Ingredients:

½ onion, diced
2 frozen chicken breasts
16 oz. chicken stock

16 oz. water
3 carrots, peeled and chopped
4 potatoes, cubed

Directions:

1. Place everything into your Instant Pot.

2. Close the lid, select MANUAL, and cook on HIGH for 35 minutes.

3. Wait 10 minutes before releasing the pressure.

4. Shred the chicken with 2 forks inside the pot.

Chicken Soup with Eggs

(Prep + Cook Time: 35 minutes / Servings: 6)

Nutritional Info per Serving:

Calories 340, Protein 26, Carbs 23, Fat 15

Ingredients:

1 lb. chicken breast, boneless and
skinless, chopped
2 carrots, peeled and sliced

2 onions, chopped
6 cups water
3 tbsp. flour

3 potatoes, peeled and chopped
2 tsp. cayenne pepper

3 egg yolks
4 tbsp. olive oil

Directions:

1. Press SAUTÉ and stir-fry the onions.
2. Add the remaining ingredients and seal the lid.
3. Press SOUP and release the pressure naturally.

Instant Pot Vegan Soup

(Prep + Cook Time: 25 minutes / Servings: 4)

Nutritional Info per Serving:

Calories 210, Protein 8, Carbs 23, Fat 9

Ingredients:

6 oz. broccoli, chopped
2 cups vegetable broth
1 garlic clove
2 tbsp. sesame oil
1 carrot, sliced

1 onion, chopped
1 cup soy milk
½ cup flour
¼ cup tofu, seasoned and crumbled
1 cup water

Directions:

1. Heat oil on SAUTÉ mode.
2. Add onion and garlic, and stir-fry for 2 minutes.
3. Add vegetable broth, 1 cup of water, carrot, and broccoli.
4. Seal the lid and press MANUAL for 5 minutes.
5. Perform a quick release, and open the lid.
6. Let cool, then transfer to a food processor. Blend until creamy.
7. Transfer the mixture back into the pot, and add the remaining ingredients.
8. Press MANUAL for 13 minutes.
9. Release the pressure naturally and serve.

Vichyssoise

(Prep + Cook Time: 20 minutes / Servings: 4)

Nutritional Info per Serving:

Calories 115, Protein 1.7, Carbs 11.6, Fat 7.3

Ingredients:

1 lb. potatoes, chopped
3 leeks, finely sliced, green part removed
5 fl. oz. silken tofu
5 cups vegetable stock
1 onion, sliced
3 tbsp. butter

2 tsp. lemon juice
¼ tsp. nutmeg
¼ tsp. ground coriander
1 bay leaf
Salt and white pepper
Freshly snipped chives, to garnish

Directions:

1. Melt butter on SAUTÉ, and add the leeks and onion. Stir-fry for 5 minutes without browning.
2. Add the vegetable stock, potatoes, nutmeg, lemon juice, coriander, bay leaf, salt and pepper.
3. Lock the lid, press MANUAL button, and cook on HIGH pressure for 10 minutes.
4. Perform a quick release.
5. Remove the bay leaf, and then process the food in a blender until smooth.
6. In a bowl, put the silken tofu and a pinch of salt, and mix well.
7. Add a little of the soup to this mixture, and then whisk it all back into the soup.
8. Press WARM (or Keep Warm) and reheat, without boiling.
9. Serve chilled, sprinkled with freshly snipped chives.

Beans Soup with Chili

(Prep + Cook Time: 35 minutes / Servings: 4)

Nutritional Info per Serving:

Calories 195, Protein 7.3, Carbs 26.5, Fat 7.1

Ingredients:

15 oz. can red kidney beans, rinsed
14.5 oz. can tomatoes
2 fresh red chilies, finely chopped
2 ½ tbsp. oil

⅓ cup tomato pasta sauce
1 cloves garlic, crushed
1 green bell pepper, diced
1 tsp. sugar

Directions:

1. Heat oil in Instant Pot, and add garlic, chili, and onion.
2. Stir fry for 2 minutes, or until translucent.
3. Add the remaining ingredients, and securely lock the lid.
4. Press MANUAL and cook on HIGH pressure for 25 minutes.
5. Allow for a natural release. Leave covered for 5 minutes before serving.

Garlicky Leek and Potato Soup

(Prep + Cook Time: 45 minutes / Servings: 4)

Nutritional Info per Serving:

Calories 198, Protein 6.7, Carbs 21, Fat 8

Ingredients:

1 ½ tsp. oregano
4 potatoes, diced
3 leeks, sliced
1 tsp. salt
1 ½ cup half and half
2 tsp. butter

2 bay leaves
4 garlic cloves, minced
4 thyme sprigs
5 cups veggie broth
¾ cup dry white wine

Directions:

1. Set your Instant Pot to SAUTÉ.
2. Melt the butter and sauté the leeks for 2 minutes
3. Add garlic and sauté for 30 seconds more.
4. Stir in the oregano, thyme, wine, broth, bay leaves, and potatoes.
5. Close the lid, select MANUAL, and cook on HIGH for 10 minutes, natural pressure release.
6. Stir in the half and half, and blend with a hand blender until smooth.

Cauliflower Soup

(Prep + Cook Time: 45 minutes / Servings: 4)

Nutritional Info per Serving:

Calories 167, Protein 11.3, Carbs 20.1, Fat 6.3

Ingredients:

1 lb. cauliflower, chopped into florets   ¼ cup cooking cream
4 cups chicken broth   fresh parsley, finely chopped
1 potato   ½ tsp. salt and pepper
1 cup milk   ¼ cup sour cream

Directions:

1. Place the vegetables, and add the chicken broth.
2. Close the lid, and set the steam release handle.
3. Press MANUAL, and set to 20 minutes.
4. Perform a quick release and open the lid.
5. Transfer to a food processor and pulse until completely combined.
6. Pour the mixture back to the Pot, and add the remaining ingredients.
7. Cook on MANUAL for 5 more minutes.
8. Release the pressure naturally.

Creamy Beans Soup

(Prep + Cook Time: 20 minutes / Servings: 4)

Nutritional Info per Serving:

Calories 175, Protein 7.9, Carbs 16.5, Fat 8.8

Ingredients:

4 cups beef broth
1 cup canned beans, cooked
1 potato, chopped
1 tsp. garlic powder

⅓ cup heavy cream
1/4 tsp. sea salt
1 tsp. ground black pepper

Directions:

1. Add all ingredients and cook on MANUAL for 10 minutes.
2. Adjust the steam release and cook on HIGH pressure.
3. Press Cancel button and release the steam naturally.
4. Transfer everything to a food processor and blend until smooth.
5. Return the soup to the clean stainless steel insert and add half cup of water. Cook on SAUTÉ for 5 more minutes.

Sweet Potato and Carrot Turmeric Soup

(Prep + Cook Time: 35 minutes / Servings: 4)

Nutritional Info per Serving:

Calories 100, Protein 4, Carbs 16, Fat 3.1

Ingredients:

3 carrots, sliced
2 sweet potatoes, chopped
3 cups veggie broth
1 tsp. turmeric
2 garlic cloves, minced

½ tsp. paprika
1 tbsp. oil
1 onion, diced
Salt and black pepper, to taste

Directions:

1. Set your Instant Pot to SAUTÉ.
2. Heat the oil and sauté the onions, carrot, and garlic for 3 minutes.
3. Stir in the remaining ingredients.
4. Close the lid, select MANUAL, and cook on HIGH for 20 minutes.
5. Release the pressure quickly.
6. Blend the soup with a hand blender.

Pork Soup

(Prep + Cook Time: 55 minutes / Servings: 4)

Nutritional Info per Serving:

Calories 331, Protein 30.1, Carbs 14.1, Fat 16.6

Ingredients:

4 pork chops, 8 oz., with bones
4 cups beef broth
3 medium carrots, sliced
2 bay leaves
2 onions, diced

2 celery stalks, diced
2 tbsp. oil
1 tsp. chili and garlic powder
1 tbsp. cayenne pepper
2 tbsp. soy sauce

Directions:

1. Press the Sauté button and grease the stainless steel bottom with oil.
2. Add onions and stir-fry until translucent.
3. Add celery stalks, carrots, cayenne, and chili pepper. Give it a good stir and continue to cook for 7 - 8 minutes.
4. Press CANCEL and the add pork chops, garlic powder, bay leaves, and soy sauce. Pour in the broth, and seal the lid.
5. Set the MANUAL mode for 35 minutes.
6. Perform a quick release and open the lid.
7. Cool for a few minutes.

Mixed Veggie Soup

(Prep + Cook Time: 25 minutes / Servings: 6)

Nutritional Info per Serving:

Calories 94, Protein 5.1, Carbs 14, Fat 2.6

Ingredients:

¼ cup chopped parsley
1 can tomatoes, diced
12 oz. frozen mixed veggies
1 onion, chopped
12 oz. green beans
2-¾cups veggie broth

2 tsp. olive oil
1 tsp. thyme
½ tsp. oregano
2 garlic cloves, minced
Salt and black pepper, to taste

Directions:

1. Set your Instant Pot to SAUTÉ.
2. Add the onion and cook for 3 minutes.
3. Add garlic, thyme, and oregano, and cook for 1 more minute.
4. Stir in the remaining ingredients, except salt and pepper.
5. Close the lid, select MANUAL, and cook on HIGH for 5 minutes.
6. Allow pressure to release naturally.
7. Season with salt and pepper.
8. Serve and enjoy!

Lentils and Tomatoes Soup

(Prep + Cook Time: 15 minutes / Servings: 4)

Nutritional Info per Serving:

Calories 326, Protein 35.3, Carbs 26.8, Fat 3.5

Ingredients:

4 cups vegetable broth

3 tbsp. tomato paste

3 garlic cloves, peeled, crushed

2 cups lentils, soaked overnight, drained

2 tomatoes, wedged

1 carrot, thinly sliced

1 tbsp. parsley, chopped

½ small onion, chopped

½ tsp. thyme, dried, ground

1 medium-sized onion, diced

½ tsp. cumin, ground

Directions:

1. Combine all ingredients in the Instant Pot.

2. Press MANUAL, and cook for 8 minutes.

3. Release the steam naturally. Serve warm.

Colorful Soup

(Prep + Cook Time: 17 minutes / Servings: 4)

Nutritional Info per Serving:

Calories 147, Protein 4.5, Carbs 15.3, Fat 8

Ingredients:

1 cup wax beans, cut into bite-sized pieces

1 cup green peas

½ carrot, finely chopped

2 red bell peppers, finely chopped, seeded

1 tomato, diced

2 cups vegetable broth

2 cups water

2 tbsp. olive oil

1 tsp. salt

¼ tsp. oregano, ground, dried

Directions:

1. Combine all ingredients in the Instant Pot.

2. Stir well and close the lid.
3. Adjust the steam release handle and select MANUAL.
4. Cook on HIGH pressure for 10 minutes.

Creamy Sausage and Kale Soup

(Prep + Cook Time: 25 minutes / Servings: 6)

Nutritional Info per Serving:

Calories 500, Protein 28, Carbs 35, Fat 35

Ingredients:

1 pound Italian sausage, sliced
3 potatoes, cubed
4 bacon slice, chopped
1 ½ quarts chicken broth
4 garlic cloves, minced

¼ cup water
2 cups kale, chopped
1 cup heavy cream
1 onion, chopped
Salt and black pepper, to taste

Directions:

1. Set your Instant Pot to SAUTÉ.
2. Add the bacon and cook until crispy. Transfer to a plate.
3. Add the onions and cook for 3 minutes.
4. Add the garlic and cook for 1 more minute.
5. Add sausage and cook for 3 more minutes.
6. Stir in potatoes, water, and kale.
7. Close the lid, select MANUAL, and cook for 3 minutes.
8. Allow pressure to release naturally.
9. Stir in the heavy cream, and season with salt and pepper.
10. Serve and enjoy!

Chicken Soup with Noodles

(Prep + Cook Time: 40 minutes / Servings: 4)

Nutritional Info per Serving:

Calories 285, Protein 38.7, Carbs 7, Fat 10.3

Ingredients:

1 lb. chicken meat, cut in pieces   salt and black pepper
4 cups chicken broth   parsley
½ cup soup noodles

Directions:

1. Sprinkle the chicken bites with salt, and place them in the Instant Pot.
2. Pour in chicken broth, and seal the lid.
3. Set the steam release handle.
4. Press SOUP and cook for 20 minutes.
5. Press Cancel and release the pressure naturally.
6. Add the soup noodles and cook for 5 more minutes on SOUP.
7. Release the pressure naturally.
8. Sprinkle with black pepper and parsley and serve.
9. Serve and enjoy!

Tomato Soup

(Prep + Cook Time: 30 minutes / Servings: 4)

Nutritional Info per Serving:

Calories 319, Protein 12.4, Carbs 34.5, Fat 15.7

Ingredients:

1 ½ lb. tomatoes, diced   2 tbsp. sour cream
1 cup white beans, cooked   ½ cup vegetable broth

1 tbsp. fresh parsley, finely chopped
1 onion, diced
1 garlic cloves, crushed
1 tsp. sugar
½ tsp. salt
¼ tsp. black pepper, ground
2 tbsp. extra virgin olive oil

Directions:

1. Grease the bottom with olive oil. Press SAUTÉ, and add the chopped onion and garlic.
2. Stir for 2 minutes.
3. Add tomatoes, white beans, vegetable broth, 2 cups of water, parsley.
4. Sprinkle with a pinch of salt, pepper and sugar.
5. Press SOUP and cook for 25 minutes on HIGH pressure.
6. Release the pressure naturally.
7. Top with 2 tbsp. of sour cream and parsley prior to serving.
8. Serve and enjoy!

Chicken and Spinach Soup

(Prep + Cook Time: 5 minutes / Servings: 6)

Nutritional Info per Serving:

Calories 181, Protein 24.1, Carbs 6, Fat 2.2

Ingredients:

½ onion, chopped
4 scallions, chopped
1 bulb fennel, chopped
2 cups chicken broth

1 pound chicken, cut into chunks
1 cup spinach
3 garlic cloves, minced
Salt and black pepper, to taste

Directions:

1. Place all of the ingredients into your Instant Pot.
2. Select SOUP, and cook for 30 minutes.
3. Allow pressure to release naturally.
4. Serve and enjoy!

Brussels Sprouts Soup

(Prep + Cook Time: 35 minutes / Servings: 4)

Nutritional Info per Serving:

Calories 191, Protein 10.3, Carbs 21, Fat 10

Ingredients:

1 lb. Brussels sprouts, halved, chopped
8 oz. baby spinach, torn, chopped
4 tbsp. sour cream
1 cup milk

2 cups water
1 tbsp. celery, chopped
1 tbsp. butter
1 tsp. sugar
1 tsp. sea salt

Directions:

1. Combine all ingredients in the Instant Pot.
2. Securely close the lid, and set the steam release.
3. Select SOUP and cook on HIGH pressure for 35 minutes..
4. Perform a quick release.
5. Transfer the soup to a food processor and blend.
6. Serve and enjoy!

Turkey and Black Bean Soup

(Prep + Cook Time: 1 hour and 10 minutes / Servings: 4)

Nutritional Info per Serving:

Calories 90, Protein 10, Carbs 13, Fat 8

Ingredients:

6 oz. smoked turkey, chopped
1 cup dried black beans
1 onion, chopped

1 garlic clove, minced
3 cups water
1 carrot, chopped

½ tbsp. olive oil   Salt and black pepper, to taste

Directions:

1. Set your Instant Pot to SAUTÉ.
2. Heat the oil and sauté the onions and carrot for 5 minutes.
3. Add garlic and cook for one more minute.
4. Stir in the remaining ingredients, except salt and pepper.
5. Close the lid, select MANUAL, and cook on HIGH for 45 minutes.
6. Allow pressure to release naturally.
7. Season with salt and pepper.
8. Serve immediately and enjoy!

Asparagus and Sour Cream Soup

(Prep + Cook Time: 25 minutes / Servings: 4)

Nutritional Info per Serving:

Calories 317, Protein 13, Carbs 16, Fat 5.6

Ingredients:

1 onion, chopped   2 garlic cloves, minced
5 cups bone broth   1 tsp. salt3 tbsp. butter
8 oz. sour cream   ½ tsp. thyme
2 pounds asparagus, chopped   Pinch black pepper

Directions:

1. Set your Instant Pot to SAUTÉ.
2. Melt the butter in your Instant Pot.
3. Add onions and sauté for 3 minutes.
4. Add garlic and thyme and cook for one more minute.
5. Stir in the asparagus, broth, salt, and pepper.
6. Close the lid, select MANUAL, and cook on HIGH for 5 minutes.

7. Allow pressure to release naturally. Stir in the sour cream before serving.

Fish Soup

(Prep + Cook Time: 45 minutes / Servings: 4)

Nutritional Info per Serving:

Calories 464, Protein 28.3, Carbs 39.1, Fat 21.5

Ingredients:

6 oz. mackerel fillets
4 cups fish stock
¼ cup olive oil
½ cup kidney beans, soaked
½ cup wheat groats, soaked

¼ cup sweet corn
½ lb. tomatoes, peeled and diced
1 tsp. fresh rosemary, chopped
salt

Directions:

1. Grease the bottom of the stainless steel insert of your Instant Pot with olive oil. Press SAUTÉ and add the tomatoes.
2. Cook for 4 minutes, stirring occasionally.
3. Add corn, rosemary, fish stock, beans, wheat groats and a pinch of salt. Close the lid and set the steam release handle.
4. Press MANUAL and set the timer to 30 minutes.
5. Once ready, perform a quick release, open the lid, and add the mackerel fillets.
6. Close again and press the FISH button. Cook for 10 minutes.

Turkey and Carrots Soup

(Prep + Cook Time: 45 minutes / Servings: 3)

Nutritional Info per Serving:

Calories 116, Protein 14.1, Carbs 9.1, Fat 2.5

Ingredients:

5 oz. turkey breast, chopped into pieces

3 cups chicken broth

2 carrots, sliced

2 tbsp. cilantro, chopped

½ tsp. freshly ground white pepper

Directions:

1. Add all the ingredients and close the lid, setting the steam release handle.
2. Press MANUAL mode and set to 35 minutes.
3. Release the pressure naturally, and open the lid.
4. Serve immediately.

Parsnip Soup

(Prep + Cook Time: 15 minutes / Servings: 4)

Nutritional Info per Serving:

Calories 110, Protein 1.7, Carbs 11.4, Fat 7.3

Ingredients:

4 cups vegetable stock

1 red onion, finely chopped

4 parsnip, chopped

2 tbsp. vegetable oil

2 garlic cloves, crushed

½ tsp. chili powder

juice from 1 lemon

½ tsp. salt and black pepper

Directions:

1. Heat oil on SAUTÉ. Add the onion, parsnips, and garlic and cook for 5 minutes, or until softened.
2. Add the chili powder and stir constantly for 25 seconds.
3. Stir in the stock and the lemon juice, and securely lock the lid.
4. Select MANUAL and cook on HIGH for 5 minutes. Perform a quick release.
5. Transfer to a food processor and blend for 1 minute to a smooth puree.
6. Return the soup to the pot and WARM for 2 minutes until piping hot.

Potato and Squash Soup

(Prep + Cook Time: 40 minutes / Servings: 4)

Nutritional Info per Serving:

Calories 236, Protein 6.4, Carbs 35, Fat 9

Ingredients:

½ tsp. turmeric

3 cups bone broth

2 tbsp. coconut oil

2 garlic cloves, minced

2 cups cubed sweet potatoes

2 cups cubed butternut squash

½ tsp. nutmeg

1 tsp. tarragon

1½ tsp. curry powder

1 tsp. grated ginger

1 onion, chopped

Salt and black pepper, to taste

Directions:

1. Set your Instant Pot to SAUTÉ.
2. Melt the coconut oil and sauté the onions for 3 minutes.
3. Add garlic, and ginger and sauté for one more minute.
4. Stir in the remaining ingredients.
5. Close the lid, select MANUAL, and cook for 10 minutes.
6. Allow pressure to release naturally.
7. Blend the soup with a hand blender.
8. Serve and enjoy!

Cheesy Broccoli and Potato Soup

(Prep + Cook Time: 25 minutes / Servings: 4)

Nutritional Info per Serving:

Calories 522, Protein 27, Carbs 23, Fat 35

Ingredients:

1 cup half and half

2 garlic cloves, minced

1 broccoli head, broken into florets

2 tbsp. butter

4 cups veggie broth

1 cup grated cheddar cheese, divided

2 pounds Yukon gold potatoes, cubed

Directions:

1. Set the Instant Pot to SAUTÉ.
2. Melt the butter and sauté the garlic for 1 minute.
3. Stir in broccoli, broth, and potatoes.
4. Close the lid, select MANUAL, and cook on HIGH for 5 minutes, perform a quick release.
5. Stir the cream and half of the cheddar cheese.
6. Blend with a hand blender.
7. Divide between 4 serving bowls and top with the remaining cheddar.
8. Serve and enjoy!

Vegetable and Side Dishes

Butter Drowned Onions

(Prep + Cook Time: 50 minutes / Servings: 4)

Nutritional Info per Serving:

Calories 20, Protein 0.3, Carbs 2.3, Fat 1.8

Ingredients:

3 large onions, sliced
3 tbsp. butter

¼ cup water
½ tsp. salt

Directions:

1. Set your Instant Pot to SAUTÉ. Melt the butter.
2. Add onions and salt, and sauté for about 8 minutes, stirring occasionally.
3. Add the water.
4. Close the lid, select MANUAL, and cook on HIGH for 20 minutes.
5. Release the pressure quickly, and set to SAUTÉ.
6. Sauté for 5 minutes to reduce the cooking liquid.

Sour Cabbage with Applesauce

(Prep + Cook Time: 20 minutes / Servings: 4)

Nutritional Info per Serving:

Calories 104, Protein 2.2, Carbs 17.5, Fat 3.7

Ingredients:

4 garlic cloves, minced
1 cup applesauce
6 cups chopped cabbage

1 cup water
1 tbsp. oil½ cup minced onion
1 tbsp. apple cider vinegar

Directions:

1. Set your Instant Pot to SAUTÉ.
2. Heat the oil.
3. Add onions and cook for 3 minutes.
4. Add garlic and cook for 1 minute.
5. Stir in the remaining ingredients.
6. Close the lid, select MANUAL, and cook on HIGH for 10 minutes.
7. Release the pressure quickly.
8. Serve and enjoy!

Carrot Beans

(Prep + Cook Time: 20 minutes / Servings: 4)

Nutritional Info per Serving:

Calories 310, Protein 15.1, Carbs 32.9, Fat 8.3

Ingredients:

2 cups cranberry beans, soaked
overnight
2 onions, chopped
2 carrots, chopped

2 tomatoes, diced
2 tbsp extra virgin olive oil
2 cups of water
fresh parsley

Directions:

1. Press SAUTÉ and heat olive oil and add onions. Stir-fry for 2-3 minutes, or until translucent.
2. Add carrots and tomatoes. Stir and cook for 2-3 more minutes.
3. Add the beans, parsley, and water. Stir and close the lid.
4. Press MANUAL and cook on HIGH pressure for 12 minutes.
5. Perform a quick release.

Vegetarian Paella

(Prep + Cook Time: 25 minutes / Servings: 5)

Nutritional Info per Serving:

Calories 243, Protein 7.3, Carbs 45, Fat 1.8

Ingredients:

1 cup green peas, frozen
1 carrot, chopped
1 cup of long grain rice, cooked
1 cup zucchini, chopped
1 cup fire roasted tomatoes

2 cups of vegetable broth
6 saffron threads
½ cup celery root, finely chopped
1 tbsp ground turmeric
1 tsp of salt and black pepper

Directions:

1. Place all ingredients, except rice, stir well and close the lid.
2. Press RICE button and cook for 10 minutes.
3. Perform a quick release and add in the rice.
4. Press MANUAL and cook on HIGH pressure for 5 more minutes.
5. Release the steam naturally.

Lentils Spread with Tomato

(Prep + Cook Time: 10 minutes / Servings: 6)

Nutritional Info per Serving:

Calories 310, Protein 18.1, Carbs 42.3, Fat 7.3

Ingredients:

1 lb. lentils, cooked
2 tbsp tomato paste
2 tomatoes, diced
1 cup of sweet corn

2 tbsp parmesan cheese, grated
2 tbsp olive oil
½ tsp oregano, dried
¼ cup red wine

¼ tsp salt   ¼ tsp red pepper flakes

Directions:

1. Grease your Instant Pot with oil.
2. Press SAUTÉ and add tomatoes, tomato paste, and half cup of water, salt and oregano and sauté for 5 minutes, stirring constantly.
3. Press CANCEL and add lentils, sweet corn, wine and another half cup of water.
4. Seal the lid, set the steam release handle and press MANUAL. Cook for 3 minutes. Perform a quick release.
5. Let cool and sprinkle with parmesan before serving.

Refried Cumin Pinto Beans

(Prep + Cook Time: 55 minutes / Servings: 4)

Nutritional Info per Serving:

Calories 236, Protein 13, Carbs 35, Fat 9

Ingredients:

2 cups veggie broth   1 tsp. cumin
2 cups water   1 ½ tbsp. shortening
1 tsp. oregano   1 tsp. salt
1 pound dried pinto beans   ¾cup chopped onion
½ tsp. black pepper   2 garlic cloves, minced
1 jalapeno, seeded and chopped

Directions:

1. Place the beans in a bowl and fill it with water. Let soak for 15 minutes.
2. Place all of the remaining ingredients in your Instant Pot.
3. Rinse and drain the beans and add them to your Instant Pot.
4. Close the lid, select the BEAN/CHILI, and cook for 45 minutes.
5. Allow pressure to release naturally.

6. Blend with a hand blender.

Cold Cauliflower Salad

(Prep + Cook Time: 10 minutes / Servings: 4)

Nutritional Info per Serving:

Calories 152, Protein 5.9, Carbs 14.1, Fat 13.5

Ingredients:

1 lb. broccoli florets	1 cup water
1 lb. cauliflower florets	1 tsp salt
4 tbsp olive oil	1 tbsp dry rosemary

Directions:

1. Rinse and drain the vegetables.
2. Cut into pieces and place them in the Instant Pot.
3. Add olive oil and 1 cup of water. Season with salt and rosemary.
4. Close the lid and set the steam release handle.
5. Press MANUAL and cook on HIGH pressure for 5 minutes.
6. Perform a quick release.

Peas with Vegetables

(Prep + Cook Time: 15 minutes / Servings: 4)

Nutritional Info per Serving:

Calories 231, Protein 6.6, Carbs 37.9, Fat 10.1

Ingredients:

1 cup green peas	2 garlic cloves, crushed
1 tomato, chopped	1 onion, sliced
4 tbsp of tomato sauce, canned	2 carrots, sliced

2 potatoes, chopped

1 celery stalk, chopped

4 cups vegetable stock

2 tbsp olive oil

Directions:

1. Add all ingredients in the Instant Pot and seal the lid.

2. Press MANUAL and cook for 15 minutes.

3. Allow for a natural pressure release.

4. Serve.

Black Bean Hash

(Prep + Cook Time: 15 minutes / Servings: 4)

Nutritional Info per Serving:

Calories 133, Protein 5, Carbs 28, Fat 9

Ingredients:

2 cups cubed sweet potatoes

⅓ cups veggie broth

1 cup canned black beans, drained

1 cup chopped onion

¼ cup chopped scallions

1 garlic clove, minced

2 tsp. chili powder

1 tbsp. oil

Directions:

1. Set your Instant Pot to SAUTÉ.

2. Add onions and cook for 3 minutes.

3. Add garlic and cook for about a minute, or until fragrant.

4. Stir in the remaining ingredients.

5. Close the lid, select MANUAL, and cook on HIGH for 3 minutes.

6. Do a quick pressure release.

7. Serve and enjoy!

Shiitake Mushrooms with Garlic

(Prep + Cook Time: 25 minutes / Servings: 3)

Nutritional Info per Serving:

Calories 301, Protein 7.1, Carbs 46.1, Fat 8.8

Ingredients:

½ lb. shiitake mushrooms
2 potatoes, chopped
2 tbsp oil
1 cup tomato sauce
½ cup onion, chopped

2 cups vegetable stock
1 large zucchini, chopped
3 garlic cloves, crushed
½ tsp chili powder
1 tbsp cumin seeds

Directions:

1. Heat oil on SAUTÉ mode.
2. Add the cumin seeds and stir fry for 1 minute.
3. Add onions, chili powder, crushed garlic, mushrooms and cook for 5 minutes, stirring constantly. Add the remaining ingredients and seal the lid.
4. Press MANUAL and cook for 20 minutes.
5. Allow for a natural release.

Garlicky Green Beans

(Prep + Cook Time: 20 minutes / Servings: 4)

Nutritional Info per Serving:

Calories 143, Protein 3.5, Carbs 9, Fat 11

Ingredients:

1 pound green beans
1 cup water
3 tbsp. olive oil
3 garlic cloves, minced

2 tbsp. white wine vinegar
2 tbsp. chopped parsley

Directions:

1. Combine the water and green beans in your Instant Pot.
2. Close the lid, select MANUAL, and cook on HIGH for 1 minute.
3. Transfer to a serving bowl.
4. In a small bowl, whisk together the olive oil, vinegar, garlic, salt, and pepper.
5. Pour mixture over the green beans.
6. Toss to combine.
7. Sprinkle with chopped parsley.

Potato Stew

(Prep + Cook Time: 35 minutes / Servings: 4)

Nutritional Info per Serving:

Calories 316, Protein 4.9, Carbs 42.3, Fat 15.3

Ingredients:

3 potatoes, chopped
2 carrots, sliced
4 cups water
5 tbsp olive oil
3 tsp tomato sauce

1 onion, chopped
1 tbsp of celery, chopped
1 tbsp of parsley, chopped
1 chili pepper, sliced
Salt and pepper

Directions:

1. Heat oil on SAUTÉ mode. Add the onions, carrots, celery, and potatoes. Stir and stir-fry for 2-3 minutes.
2. Add the water, tomato sauce, and the potatoes. Stir and securely lock the cooker's lid.
3. Set to 25 minutes on MANUAL mode.
4. Perform a quick release.
5. Open the pot and add the remaining ingredients.
6. Close the lid and cook on HIGH for 3 more minutes.

Instant Ratatouille

(Prep + Cook Time: 30 minutes / Servings: 4)

Nutritional Info per Serving:

Calories 232, Protein 4.4, Carbs 40, Fat 4

Ingredients:

1 tbsp. olive oil

1 onion, sliced

12 oz. canned roasted red peppers, sliced

28 oz. canned crushed tomatoes

1 tsp. salt

4 small zucchini, sliced

2 garlic cloves, minced

2 small eggplants, sliced

½ cup water

Directions:

1. Set your Instant Pot to SAUTÉ. Heat the oil in it.
2. Add all veggies, except tomatoes, and sauté for 3 minutes.
3. Add water and tomatoes, and season with salt.
4. Close the lid, select MANUAL, and cook on HIGH for 4 minutes.
5. Release the pressure quickly.

Quinoa and Barley with Cranberries

(Prep + Cook Time: 35 minutes / Servings: 4)

Nutritional Info per Serving:

Calories 173, Protein 7.6, Carbs 45, Fat 6.5

Ingredients:

½ cup quinoa, raw

¼ tsp. cinnamon

½ cup barley, raw

Pinch of sea salt

¼ cup dried cranberries

¼ tsp. cardamom

4 cups water

2 tbsp. honey

Directions:

1. Combine the water, barley, and quinoa in your Instant Pot.
2. Close the lid, and select the PORRIDGE. Cook on default.
3. Release the pressure naturally, for 10 minutes.
4. Fluff with a fork and stir in the remaining ingredients.
5. Serve and enjoy!

Sweet Potato and Kale with Tofu

(Prep + Cook Time: 15 minutes / Servings: 4)

Nutritional Info per Serving:

Calories 133, Protein 11, Carbs 13, Fat 2.3

Ingredients:

1 sweet potato, cubed
8 oz. tofu, cubed
2 cups chopped kale
½ cup veggie broth, divided
2 tsp. tamari

1 tsp. ground ginger
1 tsp. olive oil
½ tsp. cayenne pepper
1 tsp. lemon juice

Directions:

1. Set your Instant Pot to SAUTÉ.
2. Heat the oil. Sauté the tofu for 1 minute.
3. Add tamari and half of the broth. Stir to combine.
4. Cook for 2 minutes.
5. Stir in the remaining broth and potatoes.
6. Close the lid, select MANUAL, and cook on HIGH for 2 minutes.
7. Release the pressure quickly.
8. Stir in the kale, cayenne, ginger and cook on MANUAL for another minute.
9. Sprinkle lemon juice, serve and enjoy!

Quick Yellow Peas

(Prep + Cook Time: 35 minutes / Servings: 4)

Nutritional Info per Serving:

Calories 316, Protein 9.6, Carbs 36.4, Fat 8.1

Ingredients:

4 cups vegetable stock
2 cups yellow peas, split
2 garlic cloves, crushed
2 potatoes, chopped
2 tbsp butter

1 cup onions, chopped
1 carrot, sliced
1 tsp cayenne pepper
½ tsp salt

Directions:

1. Melt butter on SAUTÉ mode and add onions. Stir-fry for 2 minute.

2. Add the remaining vegetables and continue to cook for 6-7 minutes. Stir in cayenne pepper and season with salt, cook for 1 more minute.

3. Pour in the vegetable stock and close the lid.

4. Set the steam release handle and set to MANUAL for 25 minutes.

5. Perform a quick release and serve.

Navy Beans with Bacon

(Prep + Cook Time: 60 minutes / Servings: 4)

Nutritional Info per Serving:

Calories 190, Protein 7, Carbs 25, Fat 7

Ingredients:

1 small onion, chopped
4 oz. bacon, chopped
1 cup navy beans, soaked overnight
½ tsp. dry mustard

2 oz. dark molasses
¾cup water
¼ tsp. salt

Directions:

1. Place all of the ingredients into your Instant Pot.
2. Stir to combine.
3. Close the lid, select MANUAL, and cook on LOW for about 45 minutes.
4. Release the pressure naturally.
5. Serve and enjoy!

White Beans with Garlic and Lee

(Prep + Cook Time: 25 minutes / Servings: 4)

Nutritional Info per Serving:

Calories 331, Protein 25.1, Carbs 31, Fat 11

Ingredients:

1 lb. white beans, soaked overnight, drained
1 onion, chopped
2 leeks, chopped
2 whole garlic cloves,

1 tsp salt and pepper
1 bay leaf
cayenne pepper
oil

Directions:

1. Place all ingredients and press MANUAL for 20 minutes.
2. Perform a quick release and open the lid.
3. Sprinkle with cayenne pepper and oil, stir, and let it cool in the pot.

Tex-Mex Beans

(Prep + Cook Time: 55 minutes / Servings: 6)

Nutritional Info per Serving:

Calories 436, Protein 28, Carbs 67, Fat 5.8

Ingredients:

20 oz. pinto beans with ham
1 onion, chopped
5 cups chicken broth
1 jalapeno pepper, seeded and diced
1 packet taco seasoning

¼ cup chopped cilantro
½ cup salsa Verde
1 garlic clove, minced
Salt and black pepper, to taste

Directions:

1. Place all of the ingredients in your Instant Pot.
2. Stir to combine and season with some salt and pepper.
3. Close the lid, select MANUAL, and cook on HIGH for 42 minutes.
4. Allow pressure to release naturally, about 15 minutes.
5. Drain the excess liquid. Serve and enjoy!

Instant Steamed Asparagus

(Prep + Cook Time: 10 minutes / Servings: 4)

Nutritional Info per Serving:

Calories 84, Protein 2.5, Carbs 4.6, Fat 7.1

Ingredients:

1 pound asparagus spears, trimmed
1 ½ cup water
2 tbsp. olive oil

1 tbsp. diced onion
¼ tsp. garlic powder
Salt, to taste

Directions:

1. Pour the water into your Instant Pot.
2. Arrange the asparagus on the rack. Drizzle with the oil.
3. Sprinkle with diced onion and salt.
4. Close the lid and set the mode to STEAM. Cook for 2 minutes.
5. Do a quick pressure release. Serve and enjoy!

Sweet Pureed Carrots

(Prep + Cook Time: 25 minutes / Servings: 4)

Nutritional Info per Serving:

Calories 55, Protein 1, Carbs 11, Fat 2

Ingredients:

1 tbsp. butter

1 tbsp. honey

1½ pounds carrots, peeled and chopped

1 tsp. brown sugar

½ tsp. salt

1½ cups water

Directions:

1. Pour the water into your Instant Pot.
2. Place the carrots in your steaming basket.
3. Cook on MANUAL for about 4 minutes.
4. Perform a quick pressure release.
5. Transfer the carrots to a food processor.
6. Add the remaining ingredients.
7. Pulse until pureed.
8. Serve and enjoy!

Beets and Gorgonzola

(Prep + Cook Time: 35 minutes / Servings: 6)

Nutritional Info per Serving:

Calories 64, Protein 2.9, Carbs 10, Fat 2

Ingredients:

6 beets, trimmed

¼ cup crumbled gorgonzola

1½ cups water

¼ tsp. black pepper

Directions:

1. Pour the water into your Instant Pot.
2. Place the beets on the rack.
3. Close the lid, select MANUAL, and cook on HIGH for 20 minutes.
4. Allow pressure to release naturally.
5. Allow beets to cool until easily handled.
6. Peel and chop the beets.
7. Sprinkle with salt and pepper, and top with Gorgonzola.
8. Serve and enjoy!

Simple Garlicky Polenta

(Prep + Cook Time: 30 minutes / Servings: 4)

Nutritional Info per Serving:

Calories 200, Protein 14, Carbs 13, Fat 7.8

Ingredients:

3 cups hot water
½ cup chopped cilantro
1 ½ tbsp. chili powder
4 cups veggie stock
4 tsp. minced garlic

2 tsp. cumin
1 tsp. oregano
2 cups corn meal
1 tsp. smoked paprika

Directions:

1. Set your Instant Pot to SAUTÉ.
2. Add a splash of your hot water, the garlic, spices, and sauté for 2 minutes.
3. Stir in the rest of the ingredients.
4. Close the lid, select MANUAL, and cook on HIGH for 10 minutes.
5. Do a natural pressure release for 10 minutes.
6. Divide the polenta between 4 bowls. Serve and enjoy!

Stuffed Eggplant

(Prep + Cook Time: 50 minutes / Servings: 4)

Nutritional Info per Serving:

Calories 174, Protein 6, Carbs 25, Fat 7

Ingredients:

4 eggplants

1 lb. mushrooms, chopped.

1-½ cups water

1-½ cups grated cheddar cheese

1 cup diced celery

1 onion, diced

1 tbsp. olive oil

1 tbsp. dried basil

Directions:

1. Cut the eggplants in half and scoop out the flesh.
2. Save the hollowed out eggplants for later.
3. Pour the water into the pressure cooker.
4. Combine the eggplant filling and the remaining ingredients, except the cheese.
5. Place the eggplant mixture into the cooking liquid in the Instant Pot and cook on HIGH for 5 minutes.
6. Release the pressure naturally.
7. Divide the filling between the eggplants and arrange them on the rack, drizzle with oil, and sprinkle with salt and pepper.
8. Close the lid and cook on HIGH for 15 minutes.
9. Release the pressure quickly.
10. Sprinkle with the cheese.
11. Return to the pressure cooker and cook for 5 more minutes on HIGH.

Feta Stuffed Potatoes

(Prep + Cook Time: 45 minutes / Servings: 4)

Nutritional Info per Serving:

Calories 362, Protein 12.3, Carbs 43.9, Fat 16.5

Ingredients:

8 small potatoes, rinsed and drained
3 oz. button mushrooms, sliced
2 garlic cloves, crushed
⅓ cup feta cheese

⅓ cup olive oil
1 tsp fresh rosemary, chopped
½ tsp thyme, dried
1 tsp salt

Directions:

1. Place the potatoes in your Instant Pot. Add enough water to cover them and seal the lid. Press MANUAL for 30 minutes.
2. Perform a quick release. Remove the potatoes and let chill.
3. In a medium-sized bowl, mix olive oil, crushed garlic, feta cheese, rosemary, thyme, and mushrooms. Transfer to the Pot and press SAUTÉ.
4. Simmer until the mushrooms soften and the cheese melts.
5. Remove from the pot. Cut the top of each potato and spoon out the middle.
6. Fill with the cheese mixture and enjoy.

Potato and Scallion Patties

(Prep + Cook Time: 30 minutes / Servings: 6)

Nutritional Info per Serving:

Calories 138, Protein 5, Carbs 16, Fat 5.8

Ingredients:

9 oz. potatoes, boiled and mashed
2 eggs

1 tbsp. olive oil
⅓ cups flour

1 tbsp. sour cream
1 onion, diced
4 oz. scallions, chopped

1 tbsp. cornstarch
1 tsp. onion powder

Directions:

1. Beat the eggs and whisk them together with the mashed potatoes, in a bowl.
2. Add the remaining ingredients, except the oil.
3. Form patties out of the mixture.
4. Set your Instant Pot to SAUTÉ, and heat the olive oil.
5. Add the patties, and cook for 3 minutes per side. Serve and enjoy!

Gingery Potato and Chard Stew

(Prep + Cook Time: 20 minutes / Servings: 4)

Nutritional Info per Serving:

Calories 397, Protein 13, Carbs 33, Fat 25

Ingredients:

1 tsp. salt
1 tbsp. grated ginger
2 tbsp. olive oil
1 tsp. cumin seeds
2 sweet potatoes, cubed
½ tsp. turmeric

1 jalapeño pepper, seeded and diced
¾ cup water
1 can coconut milk
1 bunch Swiss chard
1 tsp. coriander

Directions:

1. Set your Instant Pot to SAUTÉ.
2. Heat the oil and add the cumin seeds. Cook until they start to pop.
3. Add ginger, jalapeño, turmeric, sweet potatoes, and salt, and cook for 3 minutes. Stir in the remaining ingredients.
4. Close the lid, select MANUAL, and cook on HIGH for 3 minutes.
5. Allow pressure to release naturally. Serve and enjoy!

Swiss Chard Omelet

(Prep + Cook Time: 25 minutes / Servings: 2)

Nutritional Info per Serving:

Calories 345, Protein 12.1, Carbs 14.1, Fat 27.2

Ingredients:

4 eggs, beaten

1 cup Swiss chard, chopped

1 cup heavy cream

1 potato, chopped

1 tbsp olive oil

¼ tsp salt and black pepper

Directions:

1. In a large bowl, combine the eggs, heavy cream, and potato.
2. Sprinkle with salt and pepper and stir well.
3. Grease the Instant pot and press SAUTÉ.
4. Add the Swiss chard. Cook for 5 minutes.
5. Remove the chard from the pot and transfer it to the egg mixture.
6. Add a cup of water to the Instant Pot.
7. Place the egg mixture in oven-safe dish inside the Instant Pot.
8. Close the lid and set the steam release.
9. Press MANUAL and cook on LOW pressure for 20 minutes.
10. Allow for a natural release and serve.
11. Serve and enjoy!

Bok Choy with Sesame Seeds

(Prep + Cook Time: 5 minutes / Servings: 4)

Nutritional Info per Serving:

Calories 54, Protein 3, Carbs 5, Fat 2

Ingredients:

1 medium bok choy
2 tsp. sesame seeds
½ tsp. sesame oil

1 tsp. soy sauce
1-½ cups water

Directions:

1. Pour the water into your Instant Pot. Lower the basket.
2. Place the bok choy in the basket.
3. Close the lid, select MANUAL, and cook on HIGH for 4 minutes.
4. Release the pressure quickly.
5. Chop the bok choy roughly, drizzle with the oil and soy sauce, and sprinkle with sesame seeds.

Chili Corn on the Cob

(Prep + Cook Time: 10 minutes / Servings: 4)

Nutritional Info per Serving:

Calories 59, Protein 1.9, Carbs 14.1, Fat 0.5

Ingredients:

1-½ cups water
1 tbsp. chili powder, divided
4 ears of corn, shucked

4 tsp. butter, divided
Salt and black pepper, to taste

Directions:

1. Pour the water into your Instant Pot.
2. Arrange the ears in the basket.
3. Close the lid, select MANUAL, and cook on HIGH for 3 minutes.
4. Release the pressure quickly.
5. Top each corn ear with 1 tsp. butter.
6. Sprinkle with chili powder, and salt and pepper.

Baby Carrots with Pancetta

(Prep + Cook Time: 20 minutes / Servings: 4)

Nutritional Info per Serving:

Calories 201, Protein 6, Carbs 14, Fat 10

Ingredients:

1 lb. baby carrots

1 leek, sliced

2 tbsp. butter

¼ cup white wine

4 oz. pancetta, diced

Salt and black pepper, to taste

Directions:

1. Set your Instant Pot to SAUTÉ. Add the pancetta, and cook until it becomes crispy. Add the sliced leek, and cook for one more minute.

2. Pour in the white wine. Add carrots, and season with salt and pepper.

3. Seal the lid, press MANUAL and cook on HIGH for 7 minutes. Top with butter.

Tofu and Bell Peppers in Barbecue Sauce

(Prep + Cook Time: 15 minutes / Servings: 6)

Nutritional Info per Serving:

Calories 283, Protein 13, Carbs 25, Fat 16

Ingredients:

1 red bell pepper, chopped

1 green bell pepper, chopped

12 oz. barbecue sauce

14 oz. firm tofu, cubed

1 celery stalk, diced

2 tbsp. olive oil

4 garlic cloves, minced

1 onion, chopped

Directions:

1. Set your Instant Pot to SAUTÉ. Heat the olive oil.

2. Add garlic, celery, onion, and bell peppers.

3. Cook for 2 minutes. Stir in the tofu and barbecue sauce.

4. Cook for 5 more minutes. Close the lid, select MANUAL, and cook on HIGH for 2 minutes. Release the pressure quickly.

Sweet and Nutty Polenta

(Prep + Cook Time: 25 minutes / Servings: 6)

Nutritional Info per Serving:

Calories 282, Protein 1, Carbs 25, Fat 11

Ingredients:

1 cup polenta cornmeal
½ cup honey

¼ cup pine nuts
½ cup heavy cream

Directions:

1. Whisk together honey and 5 cups of water in your Instant Pot.

2. Add the pine nuts. Set it to SAUTÉ and bring the mixture to a boil.

3. Stir in the polenta. Close the lid.

4. Select MANUAL and cook on HIGH for 12 minutes.

5. Release the pressure quickly. Stir in the heavy cream, salt, and pepper.

Spicy Eggplant with Spinach

(Prep + Cook Time: 15 minutes / Servings: 4)

Nutritional Info per Serving:

Calories 115, Protein 3, Carbs 8, Fat 6.5

Ingredients:

1 tbsp. five spice powder
2 tbsp. coconut oil

1 cup vegetable stock
½ cup coconut milk

4 cups cubed eggplant
2 cups torn spinach

1 tsp. chili powder

Directions:

1. Set your Instant Pot to SAUTÉ.
2. Melt the coconut oil.
3. Add the eggplant cubes, and cook for 2 minutes.
4. Add coconut milk and stock, and stir to combine.
5. Stir in the spinach and the seasonings.
6. Close the lid, select MANUAL, and cook on HIGH for 4 minutes.
7. Release pressure quickly.
8. Serve and enjoy!

Zesty Steamed Cauliflower and Broccoli with Orange

(Prep + Cook Time: 20 minutes / Servings: 4)

Nutritional Info per Serving:

Calories 241, Protein 3, Carbs 22, Fat 8

Ingredients:

Juice and zest of 1 orange
1 large cauliflower, broken into florets
1 lb. broccoli florets

1 tbsp. capers
4 tbsp. olive oil
1½ cups water

Directions:

1. Pour the water into your Instant Pot.
2. Add the cauliflower and broccoli in the steaming basket.
3. Set the STEAM cooking mode, and cook for 6 minutes.
4. Meanwhile, whisk together the orange juice, zest, oil, capers, and salt and pepper. Release the pressure quickly.

5. Pour orange dressing over the cauliflower and broccoli, and stir in the oranges.

Seasoned Kale with Cashews

(Prep + Cook Time: 10 minutes / Servings: 4)

Nutritional Info per Serving:

Calories 303, Protein 16, Carbs 28, Fat 17

Ingredients:

1 cup raw cashews
10 oz. kale
1 ½ cups water

½ cup nutritional yeast
1 tbsp. seasoning, any
2 tsp. vinegar

Directions:

1. Combine the kale and water in your Instant Pot.
2. Close the lid, select MANUAL, and cook on HIGH for 4 minutes.
3. Combine the yeast, cashews, and seasonings, in your food processor.
4. Process until powder forms. Transfer the kale to a serving platter and drizzle with vinegar. Top with the yeast and cashew mixture.

Buttery Rosemary Potatoes

(Prep + Cook Time: 35 minutes / Servings: 4)

Nutritional Info per Serving:

Calories 175, Protein 4, Carbs 27, Fat 4

Ingredients:

3 tbsp. butter
1½ lb. potatoes, sliced

½ cup chicken broth
1 sprig rosemary, chopped

Directions:

1. Set your Instant Pot to SAUTÉ. Melt the butter.
2. Add potatoes, and cook for 10 minutes, stirring occasionally.
3. Pour in the broth and rosemary, and close the lid.
4. Select MANUAL, and cook on HIGH for 7 minutes.
5. Release the pressure quickly.

Boiled Sweet Potatoes

(Prep + Cook Time: 25 minutes / Servings: 6)

Nutritional Info per Serving:

Calories 177, Protein 2.3, Carbs 41, Fat 0.3

Ingredients:

2 cups water   6 sweet potatoes, washed

Directions:

1. Pour the water into your Instant Pot.
2. Place the potatoes in the steaming basket.
3. Close the lid, and select MANUAL mode.
4. Cook on HIGH for 10 minutes.
5. Release the pressure quickly.
6. Serve and enjoy!

Simple Turmeric Carrots

(Prep + Cook Time: 15 minutes / Servings: 4)

Nutritional Info per Serving:

Calories 46, Protein 1, Carbs 11, Fat 2

Ingredients:

1-½ cups water
1 lb. carrots, peeled
2 tsp. turmeric
1 tbsp. butter, melted

Directions:

1. Chop the carrots into thirds. Pour the water into your Instant Pot.
2. Place the carrots in the steaming basket.
3. Close the lid, select MANUAL, and cook for 4 minutes on HIGH.
4. Release the pressure quickly. Drizzle with butter, and sprinkle with turmeric.

Lemony Artichokes

(Prep + Cook Time: 40 minutes / Servings: 4)

Nutritional Info per Serving:

Calories 77, Protein 5.3, Carbs 17, Fat 0.2

Ingredients:

2 artichokes

Juice of 1 lemon

1 lemon wedge

2 tbsp. Dijon mustard

Directions:

1. Wash and trim the artichokes, no sharp edges.
2. Rub the top of the artichokes with the lemon wedge.
3. Pour 2 cups of water into your Instant Pot.
4. Place the artichokes in the steaming basket, and drizzle with lemon juice.
5. Close the lid and select MANUAL. Cook on HIGH for 20 minutes.
6. Release the pressure naturally, about 10 minutes.
7. Season the artichokes with salt and pepper, and drizzle with Dijon.

Mushrooms and Zucchini

(Prep + Cook Time: 20 minutes / Servings: 6)

Nutritional Info per Serving:

Calories 96, Protein 5.6, Carbs 15, Fat 3

Ingredients:

1 tbsp. olive oil
¼ cup chopped basil
4 zucchini, sliced
12 oz. mushrooms, sliced

15 oz. canned crushed tomatoes
1-½ cups diced onion
2 garlic cloves, minced

Directions:

1. Set your Instant Pot to SAUTÉ. Heat the olive oil.
2. Add garlic, mushrooms, and onion. Cook for 3 minutes.
3. Stir in basil, and cook for 3 minutes. Stir in the remaining ingredients.
4. Close the lid and select MANUAL. Cook on LOW for 2 minutes.
5. Release the pressure naturally.

Balsamic Wheat Berries with Tomatoes

(Prep + Cook Time: 45 minutes / Servings: 4)

Nutritional Info per Serving:

Calories 130, Protein 3.5, Carbs 14, Fat 7

Ingredients:

1-½ cups wheat berries
15 oz. can diced tomatoes
½ cup chicken broth

salt and black pepper, to taste
1 tbsp. butter
balsamic vinegar

Directions:

1. Set your Instant Pot to SAUTÉ. Melt the butter.
2. Add wheat berries, and cook for 2 minutes.
3. Stir in tomatoes, chicken broth, and season with salt and pepper.
4. Close the lid and select MANUAL. Cook on HIGH for 30 minutes.
5. Release the pressure naturally, about 10 minutes.

6. Drizzle with balsamic vinegar. Serve and enjoy!

Italian Tofu and Tomato Bake

(Prep + Cook Time: 10 minutes / Servings: 4)

Nutritional Info per Serving:

Calories 137, Protein 11, Carbs 9, Fat 6

Ingredients:

1 block of firm tofu, crumbled
¼ cup vegetable broth
1 tbsp. Italian seasoning

1 can diced tomatoes
2 tbsp. banana pepper rings, jarred

Directions:

1. To crumble the tofu, slice it into ½-inch thick slices.
2. Place the slices on a plate, single layer and cover tightly with a plastic wrap.
3. Freeze for 3 hours or until solid.
4. Then, thaw it in the microwave on the defrost setting for around 5 minutes or until the ice crystals disappear.
5. Rub the tofu in your hands and it will crumble.
6. Place all ingredients into your Instant Pot and stir well.
7. Close the lid. Select MANUAL, and cook on HIGH for 4 minutes.
8. Release the pressure quickly.

Avocado with Eggs

(Prep + Cook Time: 20 minutes / Servings: 4)

Nutrition information per serving:

Calories 415, Protein 8.1, Total Carb: 16.3, Fats: 38.5

Ingredients:

2 avocados, halved
4 eggs
3 tbsp butter, softened
1 tbsp oregano, dried

Directions:

1. Brush the halved avocados with butter and place them in the Instant Pot.
2. Crack the eggs in each avocado half.
3. Season with salt and oregano and add 1 cup of water to the stainless steel insert of your Instant Pot.
4. Press STEAM and cook on LOW pressure for 20 minutes.
5. Perform a quick release and serve.
6. Serve and enjoy.

Poached Eggs with Leeks

(Prep + Cook Time: 15 minutes / Servings: 3)

Nutritional Info per Serving:

Calories 214, Protein 12, Carbs 11, Fat 15

Ingredients:

3 eggs
2 tbsp oil
1 cup leeks, 1-inch pieces
1 tbsp rosemary, dried

1 tsp butter
1 tbsp mustard seeds
¼ tbsp chili flakes
salt

Directions:

1. Grease the Instant Pot with olive oil and press SAUTÉ.
2. Stir-fry the mustard seed for 2 minutes, and add the leeks and butter and continue to stir-fry for 4 more minutes.
3. Crack the eggs and season with rosemary, chili flakes and salt.
4. Serve and enjoy.

Poultry

Sticky Chicken Thighs

(Prep + Cook Time: 30 minutes / Servings: 4)

Nutritional Info per Serving:

Calories 420, Protein 30, Carbs 51, Fat 18

Ingredients:

4 chicken thighs, boneless
5 tbsp. hoisin sauce
½ cup chicken stock
1 tbsp. vinegar

1 tbsp. soy sauce
5 tbsp. chili sauce
4 garlic cloves, minced

Directions:

1. Arrange the chicken at the bottom of the Instant Pot.
2. Whisk together all of the remaining ingredients.
3. Pour this mixture over the chicken thighs.
4. Close the lid, and select MANUAL. Cook on HIGH for 15 minutes.
5. Release the pressure naturally.

Salsa Verde Chicken Breasts

(Prep + Cook Time: 30 minutes / Servings: 6)

Nutritional Info per Serving:

Calories 340, Protein 55, Carbs 5, Fat 6.8

Ingredients:

1 tsp. paprika
16 oz. salsa verde

1 tsp. cumin
2 ½ lb. chicken breasts, boneless

Directions:

1. Combine the salsa and spices in the Instant Pot.
2. Add the chicken.
3. Close the lid, and select MANUAL.
4. Cook on HIGH for 25 minutes.
5. Release the pressure quickly.
6. Serve and enjoy!

Mediterranean Chicken Thighs

(Prep + Cook Time: 25 minutes / Servings: 6)

Nutritional Info per Serving:

Calories 245, Protein 35, Carbs 10, Fat 12

Ingredients:

½ lb. cremini mushrooms, halved
½ cup green olives, pitted
¼ cup chopped parsley
1 onion, chopped
6 chicken thighs, boneless
2 carrots, peeled and chopped

1 tbsp. olive oil
½ cup chopped basil
1 tbsp. tomato paste
1 tsp. oregano
Salt and black pepper, to taste

Directions:

1. Season the thighs with salt and pepper.
2. Heat the olive oil in your Instant Pot on SAUTÉ.
3. Sauté the mushrooms, onions, and carrots for 3 minutes.
4. Add garlic, and cook for 1 minute.
5. Add the remaining ingredientsClose the lid, and select MANUAL.
6. Cook on HIGH for 10 minutes.
7. Release the pressure quickly.

Sweet Chicken with Sriracha

(Prep + Cook Time: 15 minutes / Servings: 4)

Nutritional Info per Serving:

Calories 419, Protein 67, Carbs 19, Fat 7

Ingredients:

¼ cup sugar
4 chicken breasts, diced
1 tbsp. minced garlic
2 tbsp. cornstarch

3 tbsp. honey
3 tbsp. sriracha
5 tbsp. soy sauce
4 tbsp. water, divided

Directions:

1. Combine 2 tbsp. water, soy sauce, sriracha, honey, garlic, and sugar in your Instant Pot. Add the chicken and stir to combine.
2. Close the lid, select MANUAL, and cook on HIGH for 9 minutes.
3. Whisk together the cornstarch and remaining water.
4. Stir into the chicken.
5. Cook for 3 minutes on SAUTÉ.

Chicken Alfredo with Cauliflower

(Prep + Cook Time: 30 minutes / Servings: 4)

Nutritional Info per Serving:

Calories 325, Protein 22, Carbs 7, Fat 18

Ingredients:

4 chicken breasts, boneless and
skinless, chopped
4 basil leaves, chopped
4 garlic cloves, chopped
2 cups heavy cream

8 oz. cream cheese
½ cup of butter
2 cups cauliflower florets

Directions:

1. Set your Instant Pot to SAUTÉ.
2. Melt the butter, and whisk in the cream cheese.
3. While whisking, add the heavy cream. Stir in the remaining ingredients.
4. Close the lid, select MANUAL, and cook on HIGH for 15 minutes.
5. Release the pressure quickly.

Shredded Chicken

(Prep + Cook Time: 35 minutes / Servings: 6)

Nutritional Info per Serving:

Calories 240, Protein 30, Carbs 5, Fat 7.8

Ingredients:

1 ½ lb. chicken breasts, boneless and skinless
½ cup red salsa

1 oz. taco seasoning
½ cup mild salsa verde

Directions:

1. Place all of the ingredients in your Instant Pot.
2. Close the lid, and select MANUAL. Cook on HIGH for 25 minutes.
3. Release the pressure quickly.
4. Shred the chicken with two forks inside the Instant Pot.
5. Serve and enjoy!

Buffalo Chicken and Potatoes

(Prep + Cook Time: 35 minutes / Servings: 4)

Nutritional Info per Serving:

Calories 290, Protein 20, Carbs 25, Fat 12

Ingredients:

1 onion, diced
3 tbsp. buffalo wing sauce
½ tsp. garlic powder
½ tsp. onion powder
16 oz. potatoes, diced

½ cup chicken broth
1 lb. chicken breasts, cut into cubes
3 tbsp. butter, divided
Salt and black pepper, to taste

Directions:

1. Melt 1 tbsp. of the butter in your Instant Pot on SAUTÉ.
2. Add onion, and cook for 4 minutes.
3. Stir in the remaining ingredients.
4. Close the lid, and select POULTRY.
5. Cook for 18 minutes. Release the pressure quickly.

Ginger Chicken Drumsticks

(Prep + Cook Time: 65 minutes / Servings: 6)

Nutritional Info per Serving:

Calories 250, Protein 25, Carbs 21, Fat 9

Ingredients:

6 chicken drumsticks
1 cup rice
7 cups of water

1 tbsp. minced ginger
Salt and pepper, to taste

Directions:

1. Place all of the ingredients in your Instant Pot. Stir to combine.
2. Close the lid, hit MANUAL, and cook on HIGH for 30 minutes.
3. Perform a quick release.
4. Set the Instant Pot to SAUTÉ. Cook until the sauce thickens.
5. Serve and enjoy!

Honey and Ketchup Chicken

(Prep + Cook Time: 45 minutes / Servings: 4)

Nutritional Info per Serving:

Calories 457, Protein 44, Carbs 21, Fat 20

Ingredients:

3 tbsp. ketchup
¼ cup honey
2 lb. chicken thighs, boneless
1 ½ tsp. salt

¼ tsp. black pepper
2 tsp. garlic powder
¼ cup butter
¼ cup coconut aminos

Directions:

1. Place everything in your Instant Pot.
2. Stir well to combine.
3. Close the lid, and select MANUAL.
4. Cook on HIGH for 18 minutes.
5. Perform a quick release.
6. Set it to SAUTÉ and cook for 5 minutes.

Cream Cheese and Bacon Chicken

(Prep + Cook Time: 40 minutes / Servings: 4)

Nutritional Info per Serving:

Calories 700, Protein 70, Carbs 10, Fat 40

Ingredients:

1 cup water
8 oz. cream cheese
2 lb. chicken breasts, boneless and skinless

4 oz. cheddar cheese, shredded
1 ounce ranch seasoning
8 bacon slices, cooked and crumbled
3 tbsp. cornstarch

Directions:

1. Combine the water, cream cheese, and ranch seasoning in your Instant Pot.
2. Add the chicken, and close the lid.
3. Select MANUAL, and cook on HIGH for 25 minutes.
4. Transfer the chicken to a plate, and shred it.
5. Return the shredded chicken back to the pot along with the cheddar and bacon.
6. Cook on SAUTÉ for 5 minutes.
7. Stir in cornstarch, and cook for a few more minutes, until sauce is thickened.

Lemon Garlic Chicken

(Prep + Cook Time: 25 minutes / Servings: 4)

Nutritional Info per Serving:

Calories 530, Protein 65, Carbs 5, Fat 23

Ingredients:

1 onion, diced
4 garlic cloves, minced
¼ cup white wine
¼ tsp. paprika
1 ½ lb. chicken breasts, chopped

Juice of 1 lemon
1 tbsp. butter
3 tsp. flour
½ cup broth

Directions:

1. Melt the butter in your Instant Pot on SAUTÉ.
2. Add onion, and cook for 3 minutes.
3. Add garlic, and cook for 1 minute.
4. Stir in all of the remaining ingredients, except flour.
5. Close the lid, and cook on POULTRY on default.
6. Release the pressure quickly. Stir in the flour, and cook on SAUTÉ until it thickens.

Sour Cream and Tomato Chicken

(Prep + Cook Time: 45 minutes / Servings: 4)

Nutritional Info per Serving:

Calories 254, Protein 30, Carbs 6, Fat 20

Ingredients:

4 chicken breasts, boneless
1 cup sour cream
14 oz. can tomatoes, diced

¼ tsp. garlic powder
Salt and black pepper, to taste
2 cups chicken broth

Directions:

1. Combine the chicken and broth in your Instant Pot.
2. Close the lid, and select MANUAL.
3. Cook on HIGH for 20 minutes.
4. Remove from pot, and shred on a plate.
5. Discard the excess cooking liquid.
6. Set the Instant Pot to SAUTÉ.
7. Stir in all of the remaining ingredients, including shredded chicken.
8. Cook for 5 minutes. Serve and enjoy!

Chicken Thighs with Potatoes

(Prep + Cook Time: 10 minutes / Servings: 4)

Nutritional Info per Serving:

Calories 414, Protein 34.8, Carbs 35.1, Fat 11.6

Ingredients:

4 boneless chicken thighs
3 potatoes, wedged
2 garlic cloves, crushed

1 tbsp. lemon juice
2 cup water
½ tbsp. cayenne pepper

1 tsp. fresh mint, chopped
1 tsp. ground ginger

¼ cup olive oil
salt

Directions:

1. In a small bowl, add the olive oil, lemon juice, crushed garlic, ground ginger, mint, cayenne pepper, and a pinch of salt.
2. Brush each chicken piece with the mixture.
3. Grease the Instant Pot with the remaining mixture.
4. Add the potatoes to the pot, and place the chicken.
5. Add water, and close the lid. Press MEAT and cook for 15 minutes.
6. Release the steam naturally.

Artichoke Chicken

(Prep + Cook Time: 10 minutes / Servings: 4)

Nutritional Info per Serving:

Calories 373, Protein 27.4, Carbs 15.5, Fat 21.4

Ingredients:

1 lb. chicken meat, boneless, dark and white, cooked
2 artichokes
2 tbsp. olive oil
1 tsp. himalayan salt

juice of 1 lemon, divided
a pinch of chili pepper and black pepper
fresh parsley leaves

Directions:

1. Rub the meat with olive oil, and set aside.
2. Press SAUTÉ button and place the meat in the Instant Pot.
3. Cook for 1-2 minutes on each side. to get it a little golden on one side. Then press MEAT, and cook for 15 minutes.
4. Release the steam and remove the meat.

5. Meanwhile, trim off the outer leaves of the artichokes until the yellow and soft ones. Remove the green outer skin around the artichoke base and stem.

6. Remove the hairs around the artichoke heart and cut the artichoke into half-inch pieces.

7. Rub with half of the lemon juice, and place in the Pot. Seal the lid.

8. Press STEAM and cook for 4 minutes.

9. In a large bowl, mix the artichoke with the chicken meat.

10. Stir in salt, pepper, and the remaining lemon juice.

11. Sprinkle with chili pepper and parsley and serve.

Chicken with Herbs

(Prep + Cook Time: 10 minutes / Servings: 4)

Nutritional Info per Serving:

Calories 359, Protein 37.3, Carbs 12.3, Fat 16.3

Ingredients:

4 chicken thighs
3 cups chicken broth
3 garlic cloves, crushed
1 cup extra virgin olive oil, divided
3 tbsp. lemon juice

1 tbsp. fresh basil, thyme and rosemary, chopped
1 tsp. cayenne pepper
1 tsp. salt
¼ cup apple cider vinegar

Directions:

1. In a large bowl, combine olive oil, lemon juice, apple cider, garlic, vinegar, basil, rosemary, thyme, salt, and cayenne pepper.

2. Douse the thighs into this mixture, and refrigerate for 1 hour.

3. Remove the meat from the refrigerator, and pat dry using paper towel.

4. Pour the chicken broth into the Instant Pot. Set the steamer insert, and place the chicken in it.

5. Close the lid, press STEAM and cook for 15 minutes.

6. Perform a natural release.
7. Remove the chicken and the broth.
8. Grease with oil, add back the chicken and press SAUTÉ.
9. Brown for 5 minutes, flipping the thighs once.

Chicken Thighs with Tomato and Vegetables

(Prep + Cook Time: 10 minutes / Servings: 6)

Nutritional Info per Serving:

Calories 371, Protein 43.1, Carbs 12.3, Fat 19.1

Ingredients:

8 chicken thighs, boneless and skinless
½ lb. Brussels sprouts
3 medium-sized zucchinis, sliced
1 cup of chicken stock

½ cauliflower head, chopped
3 tomatoes, diced
1 onion, sliced
2 tbsp. of extra-virgin olive oil
1 tsp. of salt

Directions:

1. Press SAUTÉ and add the onion. Fry for 2 minutes and add the vegetables.
2. Continue to cook for another 5 minutes, stirring constantly.
3. Add the remaining ingredients, and seal the lid.
4. Set the steam release handle and press MEAT.
5. Allow for a naturally pressure release.

Chicken Wings in Yogurt Sauce

(Prep + Cook Time: 35 minutes / Servings: 4)

Nutritional Info per Serving:

Calories 438, Protein 36.8, Carbs 15.3, Fat 21.3

Ingredients:

4 chicken wings

2 cups chicken broth

2 tbsp. of olive oil

1 tsp. of salt

For the yogurt sauce:

1 cup of yogurt

½ cup of sour cream

2 garlic cloves, crushed

Directions:

1. Press the SAUTÉ and heat the olive oil.
2. Add the wings and brown for 8 minutes, flipping once.
3. Add the chicken broth and press MEAT for 15 minutes.
4. Allow for a natural release.
5. For the sauce, combine the sour cream with yogurt and garlic.
6. Let the wings cool for a while and top with the yogurt mixture.

Simple Leftover Chicken and Broccoli Dinner

(Prep + Cook Time: 15 minutes / Servings: 4)

Nutritional Info per Serving:

Calories 354, Protein 33, Carbs 4, Fat 24

Ingredients:

3 cups shredded leftover chicken

2 cups broccoli florets

½ cup heavy cream

⅓ cups grated Parmesan cheese

1 cup chicken broth

Salt and black pepper, to taste

Directions:

1. Place the chicken, broccoli, and broth into your Instant Pot.
2. Close the lid, select MANUAL, and cook for 2 minutes on HIGH.

3. Release the pressure quickly.
4. Set it to SAUTÉ, and stir in all of the remaining ingredients.
5. Cook for 1 minute.

Lemon Chicken Legs

(Prep + Cook Time: 60 minutes / Servings: 4)

Nutritional Info per Serving:

Calories 530, Protein 35, Carbs 34, Fat 31

Ingredients:

4 chicken legs
½ cup white wine
¼ cup triple sec
½ cup chopped celery
2 tbsp. chopped parsley
2 tbsp. vinegar

Juice and zest of 1 lemon
3 garlic cloves, chopped
¼ cup chopped shallots
¼ cup chopped carrots
½ tbsp. oil
Salt and black pepper, to taste

Directions:

1. Heat the oil in your Instant Pot on SAUTÉ.
2. Add the legs, and brown them on all sides. Transfer to a plate.
3. Add the remaining ingredients, and stir to combine.
4. Return the legs to the pot.
5. Close the lid, select MANUAL, and cook on HIGH for 45 minutes.
6. Release the pressure quickly.

Mushrooms and Chicken Thighs

(Prep + Cook Time: 30 minutes / Servings: 2)

Nutritional Info per Serving:

Calories 431, Protein 42.5, Carbs 13.6, Fat 13

Ingredients:

2 chicken thighs
6 oz. button mushrooms
2 tbsp. olive oil, divided
1 garlic cloves, crushed

½ tbsp. Italian seasoning mix
½ tbsp. butter
½ tsp. salt
½ tsp. fresh rosemary, finely chopped

Directions:

1. Rub the meat with salt.
2. Grease the Instant Pot with 1 tbsp. of oil.
3. Add the chicken thighs and 3 cups of water.
4. Press MEAT and cook for 15 minutes.
5. Perform a quick release, and open the lid.
6. Remove the thighs, drain and set aside.
7. Grease the steel insert with 1 tbsp. of oil, and add mushrooms, rosemary, and Italian seasoning mix.
8. Press SAUTÉ, and cook for 5 minutes, stirring constantly.
9. Add and melt butter.
10. Then add the chicken thighs, and gently brown them on all sides.
11. Serve and enjoy.

Chicken with Swiss Chard

(Prep + Cook Time: 30 minutes / Servings: 6)

Nutritional Info per Serving:

Calories 364, Protein 32.8, Carbs 11.1, Fat 15.7

Ingredients:

2 lb. chicken meat, dark and white
meat, cut in pieces
1.5 lb. swiss chard, chopped
3 cups chicken broth

2 tbsp. olive oil
1 tbsp. butter
1 tsp. sea salt

Directions:

1. Chop the Swiss chard and drain it in a colander.
2. Grease the Instant Pot with oil. Add the meat and pour in the chicken broth.
3. Sprinkle with salt, and close the lid. Press MEAT and cook for 15 minutes.
4. Perform a quick release. Add the Swiss chard and butter.
5. Select MANUAL and cook for 2 minutes minutes.

Raisin and Apple Chicken

(Prep + Cook Time: 25 minutes / Servings: 6)

Nutritional Info per Serving:

Calories 260, Protein 30, Carbs 14, Fat 10

Ingredients:

1 shallot, chopped
2 tbsp. butter
2 apples, sliced
1 cup chicken broth

½ tsp. dill
2 lb. boneless and skinless chicken, chopped
¼ cup raisins

Directions:

1. Set your Instant Pot to SAUTÉ. Melt the butter.
2. Add the goose, and cook until no longer pink.
3. Stir in the remaining ingredients. Close the lid, and select MANUAL.
4. Cook on HIGH for 15 minutes. Release the pressure quickly.

Creamy Chicken

(Prep + Cook Time: 30 minutes / Servings: 4)

Nutritional Info per Serving:

Calories 500, Protein 53, Carbs 17, Fat 25

Ingredients:

2 lb. boneless chicken, cut into pieces   1 bell pepper, diced

1 onion, diced   3 garlic cloves, minced

1 tsp. turmeric   1 cup coconut cream

1 tsp. paprika   15 oz. tomato sauce

1 tsp. coriander   2 tbsp. butter

Directions:

1. Set your Instant Pot to SAUTÉ. Melt the butter.

2. Add onion and bell pepper, and cook for 3 minutes.

3. Add garlic, and cook for 1 minute.

4. Add the chick and brown for 2 minutes.

5. Stir in the remaining ingredients, except the coconut cream.

6. Close the lid, and select POULTRY. Cook for 15 minutes.

7. Release the pressure naturally. Stir in the coconut cream. Serve and enjoy!

Chicken Wings with Worcestershire sauce

(Prep + Cook Time: 45 minutes / Servings: 6)

Nutritional Info per Serving:

Calories 312, Protein 41.5, Carbs 7.3, Fat 14.1

Ingredients:

6 chicken wings   2 garlic cloves, crushed

3 cups chicken broth   1 tsp. ginger, grated

2 scallions, finely chopped   1 tbsp. honey

2 tbsp. oil   ½ cups Worcestershire sauce

Directions:

1. And add the wings and the broth and sprinkle with salt. Seal the lid, and press MEAT.

2. Perform a quick release. Remove the chicken and the broth.
3. Grease with oil, add onions and garlic. Press SAUTÉ for 3 minutes, stirring constantly.
4. Add Worcestershire sauce, honey, and ginger. Cook for a minute, and add the chicken wings. Stir, and continue to cook for 2 - 3 minutes.
5. Press CANCEL and serve immediately.

Chili Thighs

(Prep + Cook Time: 45 minutes / Servings: 3)

Nutritional Info per Serving:

Calories 315, Protein 31.3, Carbs 11.3, Fat 13.1

Ingredients:

1 lb. chicken thighs

3 cups chicken broth

2 tsp. lime zest

2 tbsp. oil

3/4 cup tomato puree

1 tsp. chili powder

Directions:

1. Season the thighs with salt and chili powder.
2. Heat oil on SAUTÉ, add thighs, and brown them lightly on both sides.
3. Remove from the pot.
4. Add tomato puree, 1 tsp sugar, and lime zest. Cook for 10 minutes until a thick sauce. Return the chicken thighs, and pour in the chicken broth.
5. Cook on MEAT. Once off, perform a quick release, and serve.

Shredded Turkey with Mustard and Beer

(Prep + Cook Time: 65 minutes / Servings: 4)

Nutritional Info per Serving:

Calories 560, Protein 70, Carbs 10, Fat 15

Ingredients:

12 oz. dark beer
1 tbsp. mustard
2 turkey thighs
¼ tsp. pepper
1 tbsp. tomato paste

1 tsp. dry mustard
½ tsp. garlic powder
2 tbsp. apple cider vinegar
2 tbsp. brown sugar
2 tsp. coriander

Directions:

1. Mix the seasonings (all except the beer and the turkey in a small bowl.
2. Rub the seasoning mixture into the turkey.
3. Pour the beer in the Instant Pot, and add the turkey.
4. Close the lid, select MANUAL, and cook on HIGH for 45 minutes.
5. Perform a quick release. Shred the turkey on a plate.
6. Whisk together the remaining ingredients, and bring the mixture to a boil on SAUTÉ.
7. Stir in the shredded turkey
8. Cook for 3 minutes.
9. Serve and enjoy!

Creamy Turkey with Mushrooms

(Prep + Cook Time: 5 minutes / Servings: 4)

Nutritional Info per Serving:

Calories 192, Protein 15, Carbs 5, Fat 5

Ingredients:

1 ¼ lb. turkey breasts
6 oz. mushrooms, sliced
2 tbsp. olive oil
½ tsp. thyme
⅓ cup white wine

1 garlic clove, minced
3 tbsp. heavy cream
3 tbsp. chopped shallots
1 tbsp. cornstarch
⅔ cups chicken broth

Directions:

1. Tie the turkey crosswise (about every 2 inches) with kitchen twine.
2. Heat the oil in the Instant Pot on SAUTÉ, and brown the turkey on all sides.
3. Transfer to a plate.
4. Add mushrooms, shallots, thyme, and garlic, and cook for a few minutes.
5. Add turkey, and pour in the broth and white wine.
6. Close the lid, select MANUAL, and cook on HIGH for 15 minutes, quick release. Set the Instant Pot to SAUTÉ.
7. Transfer the turkey to a plate, untie and slice.
8. In the pot, whisk in the heavy cream and cornstarch.
9. Cook until thickened. Serve the turkey with the sauce.

Turkey Thighs with Sauerkraut

(Prep + Cook Time: 35 minutes / Servings: 6)

Nutritional Info per Serving:

Calories 454, Protein 67, Carbs 16, Fat 12

Ingredients:

¼ cup raisins
½ tbsp. red pepper flakes
2 cups sauerkraut
3 lb. turkey thighs
3 garlic cloves, minced

1 ½ cups cranberries, divided
1 tsp. cinnamon
1 tsp. flour
1 cup apple cider
Juice of ½ lemon

Directions:

1. Place the sauerkraut in your Instant Pot.
2. Top with garlic, raisins, turkey, lemon juice, and 1 cup of cranberries.
3. Sprinkle all of the spices on top.
4. Close the lid, select MANUAL, and cook on HIGH for 25 minutes.

5. Release the pressure naturally.
6. Transfer the turkey to a plate.
7. Add the remaining cranberries to the pot.
8. Whisk 2 tbsp of water and flour and, stir it into the pot.
9. Return the turkey, and cook on SAUTÉ for 3 minutes.
10. Serve and enjoy!

Simple Turkey Patties

(Prep + Cook Time: 30 minutes / Servings: 4)

Nutritional Info per Serving:

Calories 254, Protein 25, Carbs 5, Fat 15

Ingredients:

1 lb. ground turkey
1 tbsp. olive oil
¼ cup breadcrumbs
1 egg

1 tbsp. chopped parsley
¼ tsp. garlic powder
1 ½ cups chicken broth
Salt and black pepper, to taste

Directions:

1. Combine the turkey, parsley, breadcrumbs, garlic powder, egg, salt, and pepper, in a bowl.
2. Make 4 patties out of the mixture.
3. Heat the oil in your Instant Pot on SAUTÉ.
4. Add the patties, and cook until browned on all sides.
5. Transfer to a plate.
6. Pour the broth in the Instant Pot, and arrange the patties on the rack.
7. Close the lid, select MANUAL, and cook for 5 minutes on HIGH.
8. Release the pressure quickly.
9. Serve and enjoy!

Turkey Burgers

(Prep + Cook Time: 15 minutes / Servings: 4)

Nutritional Info per Serving:

Calories 345, Protein 27.3, Carbs 19.5, Fat 18.5

Ingredients:

1 lb. ground turkey
1 cup sour cream
2 eggs
1 cup all-purpose flour

½ onion, chopped
1 tsp. dried dill, chopped
1 tsp. salt and black pepper

Directions:

1. Combine all ingredients in a large mixing bowl.
2. Mix with hands and set aside.
3. Form patties with the previously prepared mixture.
4. Line parchment paper on oven dish, and place the patties.
5. Close the lid, and adjust the steam release handle.
6. Press MANUAL, and cook on HIGH pressure for 12 minutes.
7. Release the steam naturally.
8. Serve with lettuce and tomatoes.

Ground Turkey Stuffed Peppers

(Prep + Cook Time: 35 minutes / Servings: 4)

Nutritional Info per Serving:

Calories 370, Protein 35, Carbs 17, Fat 18

Ingredients:

1 ½ cups water
2 tbsp. butter

4 oz. green chilies, chopped
1 lb. ground turkey

4 large bell peppers, cleaned out
1 cup shredded cheddar
½ cup corn kernels

1 onion, chopped
2 tsp. minced garlic
1 tsp. oregano

Directions:

1. Melt the butter in your Instant Pot on SAUTÉ.
2. Cook the onion until soft. Add garlic, and cook for 1 minute.
3. Add turkey, and cook for 3 minutes. Stir in oregano, salt and pepper.
4. Transfer to a large bowl. Add the cheese, chilies, and corn to the mixture.
5. Stuff the bell peppers with this mixture.
6. Pour the water in your Instant Pot, and arrange the stuffed peppers on the rack. Close the lid, select MANUAL, and cook on HIGH for 7 minutes.

Quick Turkey Casserole

(Prep + Cook Time: 20 minutes / Servings: 4)

Nutritional Info per Serving:

Calories 454, Protein 19, Carbs 16, Fat 14

Ingredients:

2 cups cooked and shredded turkey
1 zucchini, shredded
1 cup sour cream
1 cup cooked rice
1 cup halved cherry tomatoes

½ cup kalamata olives, chopped
½ cup chicken broth
2 tbsp. diced onion
1 garlic clove, minced
1 tbsp. butter

Directions:

1. Set your Instant Pot to SAUTÉ.
2. Cook the onions for 2 minutes.
3. Add garlic, and cook for 1 minute.
4. Stir in all of the remaining ingredients.

5. Close the lid, select MANUAL, and cook on HIGH for 3 minutes.

6. Release the pressure quickly.

Seasoned Turkey Drumsticks

(Prep + Cook Time: 5 minutes / Servings: 4)

Nutritional Info per Serving:

Calories 205, Protein 24, Carbs 4, Fat 3

Ingredients:

6 turkey drumsticks
½ cup water
1 tsp. black pepper

2 tsp. brown sugar
½ cup soy sauce
½ tsp. garlic powder

Directions:

1. Combine all of the spices together, and rub this mixture into the turkey.

2. Whisk together the water and soy sauce in your Instant Pot.

3. Add the drumsticks, and close the lid.

4. Select MANUAL, and cook on HIGH for 25 minutes.

5. Release the pressure quickly.

Turkey Verde Casserole

(Prep + Cook Time: 35 minutes / Servings: 4)

Nutritional Info per Serving:

Calories 421, Protein 45, Carbs 47, Fat 4.1

Ingredients:

1 ½ lb. turkey tenderloins
⅔ cup chicken broth

1 ¼ cups brown rice
1 onion, sliced

½ cup salsa verde   ½ tsp. salt

Directions:

1. Combine all of the ingredients in your Instant Pot.
2. Close the lid, and select MANUAL.
3. Cook on HIGH for 8 minutes.
4. Release the pressure naturally.
5. Serve and enjoy!

Easy Turkey in Tomato Sauce

(Prep + Cook Time: 30 minutes / Servings: 4)

Nutritional Info per Serving:

Calories 320, Protein 27, Carbs 5, Fat 14

Ingredients:

1 lb. ground turkey
28 oz. can diced tomatoes
1 tsp. Italian seasoning
1 tsp. garlic powder
⅓ cup breadcrumbs
1 tsp. dried basil

¼ cup chicken stock
1 tsp. dried oregano
1 tsp. dried thyme
2 tbsp. onion, diced
Salt and black pepper, to taste

Directions:

1. Combine the turkey, basil, oregano, thyme, breadcrumbs, salt, and pepper.
2. Make meatballs out of the mixture.
3. In your Instant Pot, combine the remaining ingredients.
4. Place the meatballs inside and select MANUAL.
5. Cook on HIGH for 10 minutes.
6. Perform a quick pressure quickly.

Beef, Lamb and Pork

Instant Beef Bourguignon

(Prep + Cook Time: 75 minutes / Servings: 4)

Nutritional Info per Serving:

Calories 700, Protein 55, Carbs 30, Fat 34

Ingredients:

1 cup red wine
1 red onion, chopped
1 tbsp. maple syrup
½ lb. bacon, cut into small pieces
1 lb. beef, cut into cubes
½ cup beef broth

2 garlic cloves, minced
1 tbsp. oil
5 carrots, peeled and sliced
2 sweet potatoes, peeled and cubed
Salt and black pepper, to taste

Directions:

1. Set your Instant Pot to Sauté, and heat the oil.
2. Add onion, and cook for 3 minutes. Add garlic, and cook for 1 minute.
3. Add beef, and cook for about 5 minutes per side.
4. Add bacon, and cook for 1 minute.
5. Stir in the remaining ingredients.
6. Set the Instant Pot to MANUAL, and cook on HIGH for 30 minutes.
7. Release the pressure naturally, about 10 minutes.

Corned Beef with red Cabbage

(Prep + Cook Time: 110 minutes / Servings: 6)

Nutritional Info per Serving:

Calories 464, Protein 30, Carbs 17, Fat 30

Ingredients:

1 lb. carrots, peeled and sliced
3 lb. corned beef
4 cups water
3 lb. red cabbage, roughly chopped

1 celery stalk, chopped
1 onion, chopped
1 ½ pounds small potatoes
1 tbsp. seasoning by choice

Directions:

1. Place beef, seasoning, and water into your Instant Pot.
2. Close the lid, and select MANUAL. Cook on HIGH for 90 minutes.
3. Transfer the beef to a plate, and add potatoes, celery, onion, cabbage, and carrots to the Instant Pot.
4. Close the lid, and cook for 5 minutes on MANUAL.
5. Transfer to the plate with the beef.

Southern Pot Roast

(Prep + Cook Time: 120 minutes / Servings: 6)

Nutritional Info per Serving:

Calories 615, Protein 45, Carbs 11, Fat 32

Ingredients:

5 lb. beef roast
½ cup beef broth
¼ cup butter

6 pepperoncini
½ cup pepperoncini juice
1 envelope gravy mix

Directions:

1. Stir all of the ingredients except the roast in the Instant Pot, then place the beef in the mixture.
2. Close the lid, and select MANUAL. Cook on HIGH for 90 minutes.
3. Release the pressure naturally, about 15 - 20 minutes.

Sweet Short Ribs

(Prep + Cook Time: 4 hours and 40 minutes / Servings: 4)

Nutritional Info per Serving:

Calories 600, Protein 43, Carbs 76, Fat 10

Ingredients:

1 cup water

Juice of 1 orange

3 garlic cloves, crushed

½ tbsp. sesame oil

4 beef short ribs

½ cup brown sugar

¾ cup soy sauce

1 tsp. grated ginger

Directions:

1. Whisk together all of the ingredients, except the ribs, in a bowl.
2. Add the ribs, cover the bowl, and let marinate in the fridge for 4 hours.
3. Transfer the beef to the Instant Pot along with the juices.
4. Close the lid, and chose MANUAL.
5. Cook on HIGH for 30 minutes.
6. Release the pressure naturally.

Instant Pastrami

(Prep + Cook Time: 5 minutes / Servings: 4)

Nutritional Info per Serving:

Calories 80, Protein 12, Carbs 5, Fat 3.5

Ingredients:

½ tbsp. onion powder

½ tbsp. brown sugar

½ tbsp. garlic powder

1 tsp. paprika

¼ tsp. ground cloves

2 lb. corned beef

1 ½ tbsp. black pepper

2 cups water

½ tbsp. salt   2 tbsp. vegetable oil

Directions:

1. Pour the water into your Instant Pot.
2. Lower the trivet, and add the beef.
3. Select MANUAL, and cook on HIGH for 45 minutes.
4. Release the pressure naturally.
5. Coat the meat with oil, and rub the spices on it.
6. Set the Instant Pot to SAUTÉ, and cook the meat for about a minute per side.
7. Serve and enjoy!

Chili Paleo Meatballs

(Prep + Cook Time: 35 minutes / Servings: 4)

Nutritional Info per Serving:

Calories 583, Protein 51, Carbs 26, Fat 19

Ingredients:

1 lb. ground beef   ½ tsp. paprika
¼ cup arrowroot   ½ cup chili sauce
1 tsp. garlic salt   5 tbsp. grape jelly
½ tsp. chili powder   1 egg

Directions:

1. Combine the meat, arrowroot, garlic salt, and egg, in a bowl.
2. Make meatballs out of the mixture.
3. In your Instant Pot, whisk together the remaining ingredients.
4. Add the meatballs to the Instant Pot.
5. Close the lid, and cook on LOW for 30 minutes.
6. Release the pressure quickly.

7. Serve and enjoy!

Roast Lamb Leg

(Prep + Cook Time: 35 minutes / Servings: 2)

Nutritional Info per Serving:

Calories 425, Protein 46.7, Carbs 7.3, Fat 21.9

Ingredients:

2 lb. lamb leg, rinsed and dried   salt, for rubbing the lamb
4 tbsp. olive oil, for greasing

Directions:

1. Rub the meat with salt, and place it in the greased Instant Pot.
2. Add water to cover the meat, and close the lid.
3. Set the release steam handle.
4. Press MEAT and cook for 30 minutes.
5. The meat should be tender and separate from the bones.
6. Perform a quick release.
7. Serve and enjoy!

Pork Shoulder with Garlic

(Prep + Cook Time: 70 minutes / Servings: 6)

Nutritional Info per Serving:

Calories 532, Protein 39.1, Carbs 9.3, Fat 35.3

Ingredients:

2 lb. pork shoulder, boneless   2 tbsp. soy sauce
2 tbsp. apple cider vinegar   1 tsp. ginger, grated
2 tbsp. honey   1 garlic head, divided into cloves

½ tsp. red pepper flakes   1 tbsp. butter

Directions:

1. In a bowl, mix the apple cider, honey, soy sauce, and ginger. Brush the meat with the mixture, and refrigerate 1 hour.
2. Set the Instant Pot on SAUTÉ mode. Add the pork in batches and brown it on all sides. Add 1 cup of water and garlic.
3. Seal the lid and set the steam release handle. Cook on MANUAL for 35 minutes. Perform a quick release.
4. Set SAUTÉ mode. Add the meat and sprinkle with salt, pepper, red pepper flakes and butter. Cook for 15 minutes or until the liquid evaporates.

Pork Goulash

(Prep + Cook Time: 35 minutes / Servings: 4)

Nutritional Info per Serving:

Calories 413, Protein 37, Carbs 16.3, Fat 21.6

Ingredients:

½ lb. pork neck, cut into pieces	1 tsp. chili powder
½ lb. mushrooms	2 onions, chopped
4 tbsp. vegetable oil	1 medium-sized carrot
4 cups beef broth	1 tbsp. cayenne
1 small chili pepper, sliced	chopped celery

Directions:

1. Grease the Instant Pot with oil, and press SAUTÉ button.
2. Add onion, and fry for 2 minutes.
3. Add chili powder, carrot, celery, cayenne, and cook for 3 more minutes, stirring constantly.
4. Press CANCEL, add the meat, mushrooms and beef broth.
5. Press MANUAL and cook for 30 minutes.

6. Perform a quick release and serve.

Lamb Leg with Bacon

(Prep + Cook Time: 55 minutes / Servings: 4)

Nutritional Info per Serving:

Calories 421, Protein 47.5, Carbs 4.8, Fat 25.3

Ingredients:

1 lb. lamb leg

5 bacon slices

2 garlic cloves, crushed

2 cups beef broth

1 onion, sliced

2 tbsp. oil

1 tsp. rosemary

salt and black pepper, to taste

Directions:

1. Grease the bottom of your stainless steel insert with oil.
2. Add the bacon and onions in two layers. Season with salt and pepper.
3. Press SAUTÉ button and cook for 3 minutes.
4. Rub the meat with the spices and place it in the pot.
5. Press CANCEL button and pour in beef broth.
6. Close and select MANUAL for 25 minutes.
7. Allow for a natural pressure release.

New Mexico Chili Pork

(Prep + Cook Time: 55 minutes / Servings: 4)

Nutritional Info per Serving:

Calories 413, Protein 33.7, Carbs 10.1, Fat 26.3

Ingredients:

1 lb. pork shoulder

6 New Mexico chilies, halved, seeded

3 cups beef broth

2 garlic cloves, crushed

1 tsp. ground cumin

1 onion, chopped

Directions:

1. In a small saucepan, toss the chilies, and add garlic and onion.
2. Pour 3 cups of water into the saucepan and bring to a boil.
3. Once boiled, let it cool for 10-15 minutes.
4. Take the mixture from the saucepan and process in a blender until smooth.
5. Place the pork into the Instant Pot. Add in the beef broth and the pureed mixture.
6. Press MEAT button. Once done, release the pressure naturally.

Veal with Potatoes

(Prep + Cook Time: 35 minutes / Servings: 6)

Nutritional Info per Serving:

Calories 423, Protein 27.1, Carbs 31.3, Fat 23.1

Ingredients:

1 lb. veal shoulder

1 lb. potatoes, cut into chunks

5 cups of beef broth

3 sized carrots, sliced

1 onion, chopped

4 tbsp. of olive oil

¼ cup tomato paste

1 tbsp. parsley, chopped

1 tbsp. celery, chopped

1 chili pepper, sliced

salt and pepper, to taste

Directions:

1. Press SAUTÉ, and heat the olive oil.
2. Add the onion, carrots, and potatoes.
3. Cook for 8-10 minutes, stirring constantly.
4. Add the remaining ingredients.

5. Press MANUAL and cook for 40 minutes.
6. Perform a quick release and serve.

Pork Chops with Apple Sauce

(Prep + Cook Time: 55 minutes / Servings: 3)

Nutritional Info per Serving:

Calories 421, Protein 21.3, Carbs 35.6, Fat 28.7

Ingredients:

6 pork loin chops, 1-inch thick
1 tbsp. butter
2 apples, peeled, cored and chopped
1 tbsp. oil

¼ cup soy sauce
1 cup beef broth
1 tbsp. honey
¼ tsp. cinnamon

Directions:

1. Heat the oil on SAUTÉ mode and brown the chops for 4-5 minutes on each side. Remove from the Pot.
2. Melt butter and add apples, soy sauce, beef broth, honey, and cinnamon.
3. Cook until the apples are tender.
4. Press CANCEL and add the chops.
5. Set MEAT mode and cook for 35 minutes.
6. When done, perform a quick release.

Shredded Beef and Pepper Rings

(Prep + Cook Time: 75 minutes / Servings: 6)

Nutritional Info per Serving:

Calories 442, Protein 65, Carbs 5, Fat 18

Ingredients:

16 oz. jarred pepper rings
3 lb. beef
½ cup beef broth

1 tbsp. garlic powder
salt and black pepper, to taste

Directions:

1. Season the beef with the garlic powder, salt, and pepper.
2. Add the beef, beef broth, and peppers to the Instant Pot.
3. Close the lid, and select MANUAL.
4. Cook on HIGH for 70 minutes.
5. Release the pressure naturally.
6. Shred the beef with two forks.
7. Serve and enjoy!

Round Steak with Vegetables

(Prep + Cook Time: 40 minutes / Servings: 4)

Nutritional Info per Serving:

Calories 308, Protein 35, Carbs 21, Fat 8.5

Ingredients:

1 lb. round steak, cubed
4 bell peppers, chopped
1 cup of mushroom slices
4 potatoes, cubed
2 carrots, peeled and chopped

2 tbsp. butter
2 tbsp. flour
1 tsp. garlic salt
½ tsp. onion powder
1½ cups beef broth

Directions:

1. Combine the steak and flour.
2. Set your Instant Pot to SAUTÉ, and melt the butter in it.
3. Add the meat, and cook until browned on all sides.
4. Add the veggies, seasoning, and broth to the pot.

5. Close the lid, and cook on the MEAT/STEW mode for 35 minutes.
6. Drain the excess liquid before serving.
7. Enjoy!

Pork Tenderloin

(Prep + Cook Time: 55 minutes / Servings: 4)

Nutritional Info per Serving:

Calories 426, Protein 42.5, Carbs 17.3, Fat 18.6

Ingredients:

2 lb. pork tenderloin
4 tbsp. brown sugar
4 tbsp. balsamic vinegar
2 tbsp. butter

2 garlic cloves, crushed
1 cup beef broth
salt and black pepper

Directions:

1. Melt butter on SAUTÉ mode and add garlic. Fry for 1-2 minutes.
2. Add sugar and vinegar, and cook for another minute.
3. Place the meat in the Instant Pot and pour in beef broth.
4. Salt and pepper to taste.
5. Select MANUAL and cook for 35 minutes.
6. Perform a quick release and serve.

Maple Pork Chops

(Prep + Cook Time: 50 minutes / Servings: 4)

Nutritional Info per Serving:

Calories 556, Protein 37.3, Carbs 21.3, Fat 39.1

Ingredients:

2 lb. pork chops
½ cup maple syrup
2 tbsp. Dijon mustard
½ cup beef broth

1 tsp. ginger, grated
½ tsp. cinnamon
salt and black pepper

Directions:

1. Season the chops with salt and pepper. Place them in the Pot and press SAUTÉ. Cook for 3-4 minutes or until brown on each side.
2. In a bowl, mix well maple syrup, mustard, cinnamon and ginger.
3. Sprinkle the mixture over the chops and pour in the beef broth.
4. Close, select MANUAL and cook for 30 minutes.
5. Perform a quick release and serve.

Veal Shoulder with Rice

(Prep + Cook Time: 45 minutes / Servings: 4)

Nutritional Info per Serving:

Calories 541, Protein 53.1, Carbs 33.4, Fat 24.8

Ingredients:

2 lb. veal shoulder
3 cups beef broth
1 cup rice

4 tbsp. butter, divided
salt and black pepper

Directions:

1. Place the meat in the Instant Pot and add beef broth.
2. Press MEAT, season with salt and black pepper, and cook for 25 minutes.
3. Quick release the pressure and remove the lid.
4. Take out the meat, keep the broth.
5. Add the rice and 1 tbsp. of butter.
6. Close the lid, set the handle, and press RICE button.

7. Cook for 10 minutes.
8. Remove the rice and clean the steel insert.
9. Press SAUTÉ, and melt 3 tbsp. of butter. Brown the meat for 10 to 12 minutes.

Mediterranean Beef

(Prep + Cook Time: 1 hour and 40 minutes / Servings: 6)

Nutritional Info per Serving:

Calories 400, Protein 40, Carbs 2, Fat 25

Ingredients:

1 tsp. basil, chopped
1 cup beef broth
¼ cup apple cider vinegar
2 tsp. garlic powder
½ tsp. grated ginger

1 tsp. oregano
1 tsp. pink Himalayan salt
3 lb. beef
6 garlic cloves
1 tsp. marjoram

Directions:

1. Cut 6 slits into the beef, and press the garlic cloves into the slits.
2. Combine the spices and herbs in a small bowl.
3. Rub this mixture into the meat.
4. Pour the broth and vinegar into the Instant Pot.
5. Add the beef. Close the lid, and select MANUAL cooking mode.
6. Select on HIGH for 90 minutes.
7. Release the pressure naturally. Serve and enjoy!

Simple Beef with Teriyaki Sauce

(Prep + Cook Time: 45 minutes / Servings: 6)

Nutritional Info per Serving:

Calories 485, Protein 50, Carbs 20, Fat 21

Ingredients:

1 ½ tsp. grated ginger
2 lb. flank steak, cut into strips

½ cup teriyaki sauce
2 garlic cloves, chopped

Directions:

1. Place all of the ingredients in your Instant Pot.
2. Stir to coat the beef well.
3. Close the lid and select MANUAL.
4. Cook on HIGH for 40 minutes.
5. Release the pressure quickly.
6. Serve and enjoy!

Beef and Broccoli

(Prep + Cook Time: 50 minutes / Servings: 4)

Nutritional Info per Serving:

Calories 267, Protein 39, Carbs 9, Fat 8

Ingredients:

1 onion, quartered
1 lb. beef, chopped
1 garlic clove, minced
1 tsp. ground ginger
¼ cup coconut aminos

½ tsp. salt
Pinch of black pepper
12 oz. frozen broccoli florets
2 tbsp. fish sauce

Directions:

1. Place everything except the broccoli into your Instant Pot.
2. Stir to combine well.
3. Close the lid, and select the MEAT/STEW mode.

4. Cook on the default time.
5. Do a quick pressure release.
6. Stir in the broccoli.
7. Select SAUTÉ mode, and cook for 5 minutes.
8. Serve and enjoy!

Worcestershire and Vinegar Flank Steak

(Prep + Cook Time: 25 minutes / Servings: 4)

Nutritional Info per Serving:

Calories 680, Protein 55, Carbs 5, Fat 44

Ingredients:

2 lb. steak

½ cup oil

¼ cup vinegar (preferably apple cider)   2 tbsp. onion soup mix

1 tbsp. Worcestershire sauce

Directions:

1. Set your Instant Pot to SAUTÉ.
2. Heat the olive oil, and add the steak.
3. Cook until it browns. Stir in the remaining ingredients.
4. Close the lid, and select MANUAL.
5. Cook on HIGH for 25 minutes. Do a quick pressure release.
6. Serve and enjoy!

Herbed Lamb Shanks with Tomatoes

(Prep + Cook Time: 50 minutes / Servings: 4)

Nutritional Info per Serving:

Calories 700, Protein 65, Carbs 17, Fat 38

Ingredients:

1 onion, chopped

3 sprigs oregano, chopped

3 sprigs thyme, chopped

3 sprigs rosemary, chopped

2 lb. lamb shanks

2 cups tomatoes, diced

2 carrots, peeled and sliced

4 garlic cloves, sliced

6 tbsp. olive oil

1 ½ cups beef stock

Directions:

1. Set your Instant Pot to SAUTÉ.
2. Heat the oil, and cook the onion for 3 minutes.
3. Add garlic, and cook for 1 minute.
4. Add the lamb shanks and cook until they turn brown on both sides.
5. Stir in the remaining ingredients, except the tomatoes.
6. Close the lid, and select MANUAL.
7. Cook on HIGH for 25 minutes. Release the pressure quickly.
8. Stir in the tomatoes, and cook on HIGH for another 5 minutes.
9. Release the pressure quickly. Serve and enjoy!

Rosemary Lamb with Carrots

(Prep + Cook Time: 35 minutes / Servings: 6)

Nutritional Info per Serving:

Calories 670, Protein 50, Carbs 4, Fat 40

Ingredients:

1 cup sliced carrots

4 garlic cloves, minced

3 lb. boneless lamb, cubed

3 tbsp. flour

4 rosemary sprigs

2 tbsp. oil

1 ½ cups stock

Salt and black pepper, to taste

Directions:

1. Set the Instant Pot to SAUTÉ. Heat the oil.
2. Season the lamb with salt and pepper, and cook until brown.
3. Whisk the flour and stock together, and pour this mixture over the lamb.
4. Add the remaining ingredientsClose the lid, and select MANUAL cooking mode. Cook on HIGH for 20 minutes.
5. Release the pressure quickly.

Lamb Meatballs with Feta in a Tomato Sauce

(Prep + Cook Time: 25 minutes / Servings: 6)

Nutritional Info per Serving:

Calories 380, Protein 38, Carbs 17, Fat 17

Ingredients:

1 egg, beaten
1 tbsp. water
1 tsp. oregano
2 tbsp. olive oil
1 tbsp. chopped mint
½ cup crumbled feta
4 garlic cloves, minced and divided

1 ½ lb. ground lamb
1 onion, chopped
2 tbsp. chopped parsley
28 oz. can tomatoes, chopped
1 bell pepper, chopped
½ cup breadcrumbs

Directions:

1. Combine the lamb, egg, parsley, mint, feta, water, breadcrumbs, and half of the garlic.
2. Make meatballs out of this mixture.
3. Set the Instant Pot to SAUTÉ.
4. Heat the oil, and add onion and bell pepper.
5. Cook for 2 minutes.
6. Add the remaining garlic, and cook for 1 minute.

7. Stir in the remaining ingredients, and add the meatballs.

8. Close the lid, select MANUAL, and cook on HIGH for 8 minutes.

9. Release the pressure quickly.

10. Serve and enjoy!

Veggie Veal Cutlets

(Prep + Cook Time: 40 minutes / Servings: 2)

Nutritional Info per Serving:

Calories 431, Protein 31.3, Carbs 31.5, Fat 18.6

Ingredients:

4 oz. cauliflower florets

3 cups beef broth

2 veal cutlets

2 whole potatoes, peeled

2 whole carrots, peeled

1 whole onion, peeled

2 tbsp. olive oil

salt and black pepper

Directions:

1. Grease with oil the stainless steel insert of the Instant Pot.

2. Place the meat and sprinkle with salt and pepper.

3. Place the vegetables in the Pot. Add the beef broth and close the lid.

4. Set MANUAL and cook for 25 minutes.

5. Release the pressure naturally.

6. Serve and enjoy.

Mushroom Veal Steaks

(Prep + Cook Time: 10 minutes / Servings: 5)

Nutritional Info per Serving:

Calories 327, Protein 34, Carbs 7, Fat 17

Ingredients:

1 lb. veal steaks
1 lb. mushrooms, sliced
6 oz. cherry tomatoes
2 tbsp. vegetable oil

salt and black pepper
1 bay leaf
1 tbsp. thyme, dried

Directions:

1. Place the cutlets. Pour in 4 cups of water and add 1 bay leaf.

2. Press MEAT and cook for 15 minutes.

3. Perform a quick release and remove the steaks; set aside.

4. Grease the bottom of the stainless steel insert with oil.

5. Press SAUTÉ and add mushrooms and cherry tomatoes, stirring for 5 minutes.

6. Add the steaks and cook for a few minutes until brown on both sides.

7. Serve and enjoy.

Cranberry and Cinnamon Pork Roast

(Prep + Cook Time: 85 minutes / Servings: 4)

Nutritional Info per Serving:

Calories 680, Protein 45, Carbs 30, Fat 38

Ingredients:

10 oz. bone broth
2 tbsp. chopped herbs
12 oz. fresh cranberries
2 lb. pork roast
2 tbsp. apple cider vinegar

1 tbsp. honey
1 tbsp. butter
¼ tsp. cinnamon
¼ tsp. garlic powder

Directions:

1. Set the Instant Pot to SAUTÉ.

2. Melt the butter, and brown the pork on all sides.
3. Stir in the remaining ingredients.
4. Close the lid, and select MANUAL.
5. Cook on HIGH for 70 minutes.
6. Release the pressure naturally.

Braised Pork Loin in Milk

(Prep + Cook Time: 55 minutes / Servings: 4)

Nutritional Info per Serving:

Calories 380, Protein 45, Carbs 4, Fat 19

Ingredients:

1 bay leaf
2 ½ cups milk
2 tsp. salt

1 tsp. black pepper
2 tbsp. olive oil
2 lb. pork loin

Directions:

1. Set the Instant Pot to SAUTÉ.
2. Heat the oil, and brown the pork on all sides.
3. Season with salt and pepper.
4. Add the milk and bay leaf.
5. Close the lid, and select MANUAL.
6. Cook on HIGH for 30 minutes.
7. Wait 10 minutes before releasing the pressure quickly.
8. Serve and enjoy!

Creamy Pork Sausage

(Prep + Cook Time: 35 minutes / Servings: 4)

Nutritional Info per Serving:

Calories 500, Protein 25, Carbs 17, Fat 30

Ingredients:

1 lb. pork sausage

4 garlic cloves, minced

¼ cup flour

2 cups milk, divided

Directions:

1. Grease the Instant Pot with cooking spray, and set it to SAUTÉ.
2. Add garlic, and cook for 1 minute.
3. Add sausage, and cook until brown, breaking it with a spatula as it cooks.
4. Pour in 1½ cups of the milk.
5. Close, and select MANUAL. Cook on HIGH for 5 minutes.
6. Release the pressure quickly.
7. Whisk together the remaining milk and flour.
8. Turn the SAUTÉ mode on, and pour this mixture over the sausage.
9. Cook for 5 minutes.
10. Serve and enjoy!

Sour Cream and Onion Pork Chops

(Prep + Cook Time: 30 minutes / Servings: 4)

Nutritional Info per Serving:

Calories 485, Protein 37, Carbs 11, Fat 28

Ingredients:

1. 10 oz. chicken broth
   10 oz. French onion soup, condensed

½ cup sour cream

4 pork chops

Directions:

1. Add broth, and pork chops in the Instant Pot.
2. Close the lid, select MANUAL, and cook on HIGH for 12 minutes.
3. Release the pressure naturally.
4. Whisk together the soup and sour cream, and pour this mixture over the pork chops.
5. Turn to SAUTÉ, and cook for 7 more minutes.

Instant Pork Belly

(Prep + Cook Time: 5 minutes / Servings: 4)

Nutritional Info per Serving:

Calories 610, Protein 30, Carbs 0, Fat 60

Ingredients:

1 lb. pork belly
1 rosemary sprig
½ cup white wine

1 garlic clove
3 tbsp. olive oil
Salt and black pepper, to taste

Directions:

1. Add the oil to your Instant Pot, and heat it on SAUTÉ.
2. Add pork, and sear for about 3 minutes per side.
3. Add the remaining ingredients.
4. Bring to a boil on SAUTÉ.
5. Switch to MANUAL, close the lid, and cook on HIGH for 40 minutes.
6. Release the pressure quickly. Serve and enjoy!

Pork Butt

(Prep + Cook Time: 1 hour and 15 minutes / Servings: 6)

Nutritional Info per Serving:

Calories 800, Protein 60, Carbs 1, Fat 55

Ingredients:

4 lb. pork butt

3 cups water

1 tbsp. oil

2 tsp. cumin

2 tsp. sugar

2 tsp. oregano

2 tsp. paprika

2 tsp. black pepper

1 tsp. cayenne pepper

Directions:

1. Brush the oil over the pork.
2. Combine the spices in a small bowl, and rub this mixture into the meat.
3. Pour water in your Instant Pot.
4. Add the seasoned pork, and close the lid.
5. Select MANUAL, and cook on HIGH for 65 minutes.
6. Release the pressure quickly. Serve and enjoy!

Pulled Barbecue Pork

(Prep + Cook Time: 105 minutes / Servings: 4)

Nutritional Info per Serving:

Calories 780, Protein 120, Carbs 5, Fat 30

Ingredients:

¼ cup vegetable oil

2 ½ lb. pork roast

2 cups chicken stock

8 oz. barbecue sauce

Salt and black pepper, to taste

Directions:

1. Season the pork with salt and pepper.
2. Heat the oil on SAUTÉ in your Instant Pot.
3. Add the pork, and cook for 3 minutes per side.

4. Add the stock, and close the lid.
5. Select MEAT/STEW, and cook for 90 minutes.
6. Release the pressure quickly.
7. Shred the meat with two forks.
8. Add the barbecue sauce, and stir to combine.
9. Close the lid, and select MANUAL.
10. Cook on HIGH for 5 minutes.

Sweet Mustard Pork Chops

(Prep + Cook Time: 25 minutes / Servings: 4)

Nutritional Info per Serving:

Calories 800, Protein 50, Carbs 20, Fat 55

Ingredients:

2 lb. pork chops
2 tbsp. Dijon mustard
¼ cup honey
¼ tsp. black pepper
½ tsp. cinnamon
½ tbsp. maple syrup
½ tsp. grated ginger
½ tsp. salt

Directions:

1. Season the pork chops with salt and pepper.
2. Grease the Instant Pot with cooking spray.
3. Brown the pork chops on SAUTÉ on all sides.
4. In a bowl, whisk together the remaining ingredients.
5. Pour the mixture over the pork.
6. Close the lid, select MANUAL, and cook on HIGH for 15 minutes.
7. Release the pressure quickly.
8. Serve and enjoy!

Pork in Creamy Mushroom Sauce

(Prep + Cook Time: 35 minutes / Servings: 4)

Nutritional Info per Serving:

Calories 380, Protein 19, Carbs 1, Fat 30

Ingredients:

1 can cream of mushroom soup   1 ½ cups water
4 pork chops   2 tbsp. oil

Directions:

1. Heat the oil in your Instant Pot on SAUTÉ.
2. Add pork, and cook until browned on all sides. Transfer to a platter.
3. Pour water, and deglaze the pot.
4. Return the pork, and pour the mushroom soup over the chops.
5. Close the lid, and select MANUAL.
6. Cook on HIGH for 18 minutes.
7. Release the pressure naturally, about 10 minutes.
8. Serve and enjoy!

Pork Ribs and Sauerkraut

(Prep + Cook Time: 40 minutes / Servings: 6)

Nutritional Info per Serving:

Calories 400, Protein 28, Carbs 8.4, Fat 26.8

Ingredients:

1 tbsp. brown sugar   1 tbsp. oil
1 lb. pork ribs   24 oz. sauerkraut
¼ tsp. black pepper   ½ tsp. salt
14 oz. kielbasa, sliced

Directions:

1. Heat the oil in your Instant Pot on SAUTÉ.
2. Add pork ribs, and cook until browned.
3. Sprinkle with salt and pepper.
4. Stir in the remaining ingredients.
5. Close the lid, and select MANUAL.
6. Cook on HIGH for 15 minutes.
7. Release the pressure naturally, about 10 minutes.

Veggie Chowder

(Prep + Cook Time: 35 minutes / Servings:)

Nutritional Info per Serving:

Calories 266, Protein 5, Carbs 38, Fat 11

Ingredients:

1 cup coconut milk

1 tbsp. potato starch

3 carrots, peeled and chopped

3 ½ cups corn

3 potatoes, chopped

3 garlic cloves, minced

4 cups vegetable broth

1 tbsp. coconut oil

1 tsp. paprika

½ tsp. cumin

1 onion, diced

Salt and black pepper, to taste

Directions:

1. Set your Instant Pot to SAUTÉ.
2. Melt the coconut oil.
3. Add onions and corn, and cook for 3 minutes.
4. Add garlic and cook for one minute.
5. Stir in cumin, paprika, broth, carrots, and potatoes.
6. Season with salt and pepper.
7. Close the Instant Pot and set the cooking time to MANUAL.
8. Cook on HIGH for 6 minutes.
9. Release the pressure naturally, for 15 minutes.
10. Serve and enjoy!

Tomato, Bell Pepper and Lentil Chili

(Prep + Cook Time: 35 minutes / Servings: 6)

Nutritional Info per Serving:

Calories 320, Protein 20, Carbs 58, Fat 3

Ingredients:

1 onion, chopped	1 tsp. salt
28 oz. tomatoes, diced	2 tbsp. olive oil
1 cup red lentils	¼ tsp. pepper
1 ⅔ cups French or brown lentils	2 tsp. cumin
2 bell peppers, chopped	7 cups veggie stock
2 tsp. minced garlic	1 tbsp. chili powder

Directions:

1. Set your Instant Pot to SAUTÉ.
2. Heat the oil and sauté the onions and peppers for 4 minutes.
3. Add garlic and cook for 1 minute.
4. Stir in the remaining ingredients.
5. Close the lid, set the cooking mode to MANUAL.
6. Cook on HIGH for 18 minutes.
7. Release the pressure naturally for 10 minutes.
8. Serve and enjoy!

Red Bean and Plantain Stew

(Prep + Cook Time: 80 minutes / Servings: 4)

Nutritional Info per Serving:

Calories 110, Protein 4, Carbs 13, Fat 3

Ingredients:

2 carrots, chopped
1 plantain, chopped
1 tomato, chopped
½ lb. dry red beans
½ onion, chopped

1 ½ tbsp. oil
1 green onion, sliced
Water, as needed
Salt and pepper, to taste

Directions:

1. Set your Instant Pot to SAUTÉ mode.
2. Heat the oil, and sauté the onions for about 3 minutes.
3. Add beans and pour enough water to cover.
4. Close the Instant Pot, select MANUAL, and cook on HIGH for 30 minutes.
5. Release the pressure naturally.
6. Stir in the remaining ingredients.
7. Close the lid, and cook on HIGH for another 30 minutes.
8. Do a natural pressure release.
9. Serve and enjoy!

Potato Creamy Stew

(Prep + Cook Time: 45 minutes / Servings: 3)

Nutritional Info per Serving:

Calories 302, Protein 6.5, Carbs 31 Fat 14.3

Ingredients:

1 lb. potatoes, peeled, cut into pieces
2 carrots, sliced
3 celery stalks, chopped
2 cups vegetable broth
2 tbsp olive oil
2 onions, chopped

1 zucchini, half-inch thick slices
1 tbsp cayenne pepper
1 tsp sea salt and black pepper
1 bay leaves

Directions:

1. Press SAUTÉ, heat the oil and add the onions. Stir fry until translucent.
2. Add carrots, zucchini, celery stalks, and half cup of vegetable broth.
3. Cook for 10 minutes, stirring constantly.
4. Add potatoes, cayenne pepper, salt, pepper, and bay leaves.
5. Seal the lid and press the STEW button.
6. Set the pressure release handle and cook for 30 minutes.
7. Allow for a natural pressure release and serve.

Mushroom Stew with Peas

(Prep + Cook Time: 35 minutes / Servings: 3)

Nutritional Info per Serving:

Calories 254, Protein 6.9, Carbs 43.7, Fat 6.5

Ingredients:

5 oz. Portobello mushrooms, sliced
2 cups vegetable stock
2 potatoes, chopped
½ cup green peas
½ onion, minced
2 tbsp butter
1 large carrot

½ cup celery stalks, chopped
2 garlic cloves, crushed
1 tbsp apple cider vinegar
1 tsp rosemary
1 tbsp cayenne pepper
½ tsp salt and black pepper

Directions:

1. Sauté onions, carrots, celery stalks, and garlic on SAUTÉ mode for a few minutes..
2. Season with salt, pepper, rosemary, and cayenne pepper.
3. Add the remaining ingredients and seal the lid.
4. Set the steam release handle and press MANUAL and time to 30 minutes.
5. Allow for a natural pressure release.

Pressure Cooked Chili Con Carne

(Prep + Cook Time: 30 minutes / Servings: 6)

Nutritional Info per Serving:

Calories 770, Protein 65, Carbs 90, Fat 2

Ingredients:

2 tbsp. minced garlic

28 oz. can crushed tomatoes

14 oz. can kidney beans

14 oz. can black beans

1 ½ lb. ground beef

1 tbsp. chili powder

1 tsp. oregano

1 jalapeño, seeded and diced

½ cup chopped red bell pepper

½ cup water

1 tbsp. Worcestershire sauce

½ tsp. pepper

1 ½ cups diced onion

1 tsp. salt

3 tbsp. olive oil

Directions:

1. Set your Instant Pot to SAUTÉ.

2. Heat the oil and add the onions. Cook for 3 minutes.

3. Add garlic and beef, and brown beef.

4. Stir in bell pepper and jalapeños, and cook for 3 minutes.

5. Stir in all of the remaining ingredients.

6. Close the Instant Pot, and set the mode to MANUAL.

7. Cook on HIGH for 10 minutes.

8. Release the pressure for 10 minutes.

9. Serve and enjoy!

Citrus Chicken Stew

(Prep + Cook Time: 45 minutes / Servings: 3)

Nutritional Info per Serving:

Calories 316, Protein 31.4, Carbs 12.7, Fat 9.3

Ingredients:

1 lb. chicken breast, boneless and skinless

1 cup fire roasted tomatoes, diced

1 tbsp. chili powder

2 cups chicken broth

juice from 1 orange

Directions:

1. Sprinkle the meat with salt and pepper, and place it in the Instant Pot.
2. Add the remaining ingredients, except the orange juice and the chicken broth. Press SAUTÉ and cook for 10 minutes, stirring occasionally.
3. Press CANCEL, and pour in the chicken broth and orange juice.
4. Seal the lid, and set the steam release handle.
5. Press MEAT and cook for 25 minutes.
6. Allow for a natural pressure release and serve immediately.

Spicy Chicken Curry

(Prep + Cook Time: 35 minutes / Servings: 4)

Nutritional Info per Serving:

Calories 619, Protein 32, Carbs, Fat 7

Ingredients:

1 can corn, undrained

1 can diced tomatoes, undrained

1 tbsp. curry powder

2 tsp. cumin

2 tsp. chili powder

1 can beans, drained

1 lb. chicken breasts, cut into chunks

2 cups chicken broth

Directions:

1. Place all of the ingredients into your Instant Pot.
2. Stir to combine well.
3. Close the lid and select MANUAL cooking mode.
4. Cook on HIGH for 20 minutes.
5. Release the pressure naturally, about 10 minutes.
6. Shred the chicken with two forks, inside the Instant Pot.
7. Serve and enjoy!

Veal Stew with Mushrooms

(Prep + Cook Time: 55 minutes / Servings: 6)

Nutritional Info per Serving:

Calories 370, Protein 38.3, Carbs 11.5, Fat 20.5

Ingredients:

1 lb. veal cuts, chopped into pieces
1 lb. chicken breasts, boneless, skinless, cut into pieces
10 oz. button mushrooms, sliced
4 carrots, sliced

4 oz. celery root, chopped
3 tbsp. butter, softened
1 tbsp. olive oil
1 tbsp. cayenne pepper
½ tsp. salt and black pepper

Directions:

1. Grease the bottom of the Instant Pot with olive oil.
2. Add the veal chops, carrots, celery root, salt, cayenne and black pepper.
3. Stir, add 2 cups of water.
4. Close, set the handle, and press MEAT button. Cook for 15 minutes.
5. Then add the chicken breast, butter, and 1 more cup of water.
6. Simmer for 20 minutes, or until tender and fully cooked.
7. Add the mushrooms and cook for 10 more minutes. Serve warm.

Turkey Chili

(Prep + Cook Time: 60 minutes / Servings: 4)

Nutritional Info per Serving:

Calories 700, Protein 64, Carbs 79, Fat 26

Ingredients:

1 tbsp. olive oil
½ tsp. oregano
1 onion, chopped
¼ cup hot sauce
4 garlic cloves, minced
1 cup grated cheddar cheese

1 can beans, drained
1 can crushed tomatoes, undrained
1 tsp. cumin
1 lb. ground turkey
2 bell peppers, chopped

Directions:

1. Set your Instant Pot to SAUTÉ. Heat the olive oil.
2. Add onion and peppers, and cook for 5 minutes.
3. Add garlic and sauté for 2 minutes. Add in spices and tureky aand sauté for cook for 6 - 7 minutes. Stir in the remaining ingredients, except the cheese.
4. Close the lid and select the BEANS/CHILI cooking mode.
5. Cook on the default setting. Release the pressure naturally.
6. Serve topped with the cheese.

Cheesy Buffalo Chicken Stew

(Prep + Cook Time: 20 minutes / Servings: 4)

Nutritional Info per Serving:

Calories 528, Protein 35, Carbs 4.1, Fat 40.9

Ingredients:

¼ cup diced onion

2 tbsp. butter

1 tbsp. ranch dressing mix
1 garlic clove, minced
½ cup diced celery
2 cups grated cheddar cheese
2 chicken breasts, boneless and

skinless
1 ½ cups chicken broth
1 cup heavy cream
⅓ cup hot sauce

Directions:

1. Place everything except the cream and cheddar into the Instant Pot.

2. Close the lid and select MANUAL. Cook on HIGH for 15 minutes.

3. Release the pressure naturally.

4. Shred the chicken inside the Instant Pot. Stir in the cream and cheese.

5. Serve and enjoy!

Fish Stew

(Prep + Cook Time: 30 minutes / Servings: 6)

Nutritional Info per Serving:

Calories 453, Protein 38.1, Carbs 11.3, Fat 24.1

Ingredients:

2 lb. fish and seafood, any kind
¼ cup olive oil, divided
2 onions, peeled and chopped

2 carrots, grated
fresh parsley
2 garlic cloves, crushed

Directions:

1. Grease the bottom of the Instant Pot with 3 tbsp. olive oil.

2. Press SAUTÉ and add onion and garlic. Stir-fry for 3 minutes, or until translucent.

3. Add the remaining ingredients and close the lid.

4. Set the steam release handle and press MANUAL button.

5. Cook for 12 minutes. Perform a quick release.

Shrimp Stew

(Prep + Cook Time: 35 minutes / Servings: 6)

Nutritional Info per Serving:

Calories 235, Protein 18.5, Carbs 25.5, Fat 11.3

Ingredients:

1 lb. shrimp, cleaned
4 oz. Brussels sprouts
4 oz. whole okra
2 carrots, sliced
2 cups chicken broth
2 tomatoes, diced

2 tbsp. tomato paste
1 cup olive oil
½ cup balsamic vinegar
½ tbsp. chili powder
1 tbsp. fresh rosemary, chopped
sea salt and black pepper

Directions:

1. In a large bowl, combine olive oil, rosemary, balsamic vinegar, salt and black pepper. Stir well and add the shrimp to the bowl.
2. Toss well to coat and cool in the fridge for 25 minutes.
3. Meanwhile, remove the outer layers of the Brussels sprouts and slice the carrots.
4. Place the diced tomatoes in the Instant Pot, and add tomato paste, 2 tbsp. olive oil and chili powder.
5. Press SAUTÉ and cook for 6 minutes, stirring continuously.
6. Transfer the sauce to a bowl and cover.
7. Pour the chicken broth into your Pot and add Brussels sprouts, carrots, okra, salt, pepper and close the lid.
8. Set the steam release handle and cook on MANUAL for 15 minutes.
9. Perform a quick release, and remove the vegetables.
10. Place the shrimp in the remaining broth. Seal the lid, set the steam release, click on FISH button and cook for 3 minutes.
11. Perform a quick release and set aside.

12. Heat the remaining oil in a large saucepan on high heat.

13. Add the cooked vegetables, stir well and cook for 3 minutes.

14. Remove from the heat and transfer to a serving bowl.

15. Add the shrimp and the tomato sauce. Drizzle with the marinade and serve.

Classic Beef Stew

(Prep + Cook Time: 35 minutes / Servings: 4)

Nutritional Info per Serving:

Calories 428, Protein 46.3, Carbs 21.5, Fat 14.5

Ingredients:

1 lb. beef
1 sweet potato, cut into chunks
½ cup red wine
3 cups beef broth
4 oz. baby carrots, sliced
4 oz. tomato paste

1 onion, chopped
½ cup green peas
1 tbsp. bacon grease
2 garlic cloves, crushed
1 tsp. thyme, dried
1 bay leaf

Directions:

1. Grease the bottom of the Pot with bacon grease.

2. Add the beef and press SAUTÉ for 10 minutes.

3. Add onion and garlic. Continue to cook for 5 minutes, stirring constantly.

4. Add the other ingredients, and seal the lid.

5. Press MEAT for 20 minutes. When done, perform a quick release.

Potato and Bacon Chowder

(Prep + Cook Time: 15 minutes / Servings: 6)

Nutritional Info per Serving:

Calories 629, Protein 27, Carbs 49, Fat 15

Ingredients:

1 cup heavy cream
4 lb. russet potatoes
¼ cup butter
3 cups chicken stock
14 oz. bacon, cooked and chopped

¼ cup milk
2 celery stalks, chopped
1 tbsp. seasoning salt
1 garlic clove, minced
1 medium onion, diced

Directions:

1. Combine all of the ingredients in your Instant Pot, except the milk.

2. Close the lid and select MANUAL cooking mode.

3. Cook on HIGH for 5 minutes. Release the pressure quickly.

4. Mash the potatoes roughly, with a potato masher, inside the Instant Pot.

5. Stir in the milk. Serve and enjoy!

Pork Shoulder Stew

(Prep + Cook Time: 65 minutes / Servings: 6)

Nutritional Info per Serving:

Calories 650, Protein 65, Carbs 25, Fat 25

Ingredients:

1 lb. string beans
1 tbsp. cumin
2 tbsp. curry powder
4 carrots, peeled and sliced
2 celery root, chopped
2 cups broth

2 lb. pork shoulder, cut into cubes
2 garlic cloves, minced
14 oz. coconut milk
1 can diced tomatoes
1 onion, diced

Directions:

1. Place all ingredients into your Instant Pot. Stir to combine.

2. Set to STEW mode. Once ready, release the pressure naturally.

Peanut Butter and Pineapple Stew

(Prep + Cook Time: 35 minutes / Servings: 4)

Nutritional Info per Serving:

Calories 450, Protein 15, Carbs 26, Fat 20

Ingredients:

½ cup peanut butter
1 cup brown rice
1 tsp. black pepper
2 tsp. red pepper flakes
2 tbsp. olive oil

4 cups veggie stock
2 cups pineapple chunks
2 tbsp. diced shallot
3 cups torn spinach
½ cup chopped cilantro

Directions:

1. Set your Instant Pot to SAUTÉ. Heat the oil.
2. Add shallots, salt, black and red pepper, and cook for 2 minutes.
3. Stir in rice, peanut butter, and stock.
4. Close the lid, select MANUAL, and cook on HIGH for 15 minutes.
5. Release the pressure quickly. Stir in the remaining ingredients.
6. Cook on MANUAL for 2 more minutes. Release the pressure naturally.
7. Serve and enjoy!

Veggie Tarragon Stew

(Prep + Cook Time: 25 minutes / Servings: 4)

Nutritional Info per Serving:

Calories 354, Protein 13, Carbs 38, Fat 12

Ingredients:

1 onion, diced
2 cups chopped parsnInstant Pots

4 carrots, peeled and chopped
4 tomatoes, chopped

1 tbsp. chopped tarragon
2 tbsp. olive oil
3 garlic cloves, minced
4 cups veggie stock

2 cups cubed red potatoes
1 cup chopped red bell peppers
1 cup cubed beets
Salt and black pepper, to taste

Directions:

1. Set your Instant Pot to SAUTÉ. Heat the olive oil.
2. Add garlic and onion, and cook for 3 minutes.
3. Add the other veggies, and cook for 3 minutes.
4. Pour the broth in, and season with salt and pepper.
5. Close the lid and select the MANUAL mode.
6. Cook on HIGH for 7 minutes. Release the pressure naturally.
7. Serve and enjoy!

Worcestershire Beef Chili

(Prep + Cook Time: 55 minutes / Servings: 4)

Nutritional Info per Serving:

Calories 308, Protein 37, Carbs 21, Fat 9

Ingredients:

1 lb. ground beef
1 tbsp. Worcestershire sauce
1 tsp. salt
1 tbsp. chopped parsley
½ tsp. pepper
4 carrots, sliced
26 oz. can tomatoes, diced

4 tsp. chili powder
1 tbsp. oil
1 tsp. onion powder
1 tsp. garlic powder
1 bell pepper, chopped
1 onion, chopped
1 tsp. paprika

Directions:

1. Set your Instant Pot to SAUTÉ.
2. Heat the oil and cook the beef until browned.

3. Add onion, salt, pepper, chili, onion and garlic powders, paprika, and cook for 2 minutes
4. Stir in the remaining ingredients.
5. Close the lid and select the STEW cooking mode.
6. Select the default cooking time.
7. Release the pressure naturally.
8. Serve and enjoy!

Creamy Fish Stew

(Prep + Cook Time: 20 minutes / Servings: 6)

Nutritional Info per Serving:

Calories 165, Protein 24, Carbs 6, Fat 12

Ingredients:

1 onion, diced
4 carrots, peeled and sliced
4 potatoes, cubed
1 lb. white fish fillets
3 cups fish broth
2 tbsp. butter

2 celery stalks, chopped
1 bay leaf
1 cup heavy cream
1 cup frozen corn
Salt and black pepper, to taste

Directions:

1. Set the Instant Pot to SAUTÉ. Melt the butter.
2. Add onions, and cook for 3 minutes.
3. Stir in the remaining ingredients, except the heavy cream.
4. Close the lid and select MANUAL. Cook on HIGH for 4 minutes.
5. Release the pressure naturally.
6. Discard the bay leaf and stir in the heavy cream.
7. Serve and enjoy!

Ginger Stew

(Prep + Cook Time: 30 minutes / Servings: 4)

Nutritional Info per Serving:

Calories 221, Protein 7.1, Carbs 16.3, Fat 13.9

Ingredients:

2 cups green peas
3 gloves garlic, chopped
2 tbsp olive oil
1 onion, chopped

1 tbsp ginger powder
1 tbsp turmeric
1 tbsp salt
3 cups beef stock

Directions:

1. Heat oil on SAUTÉ mode. Fry the onions and garlic for 3 minutes, stirring constantly. Add the remaining ingredients and seal the lid.

2. Set the steam handle and press STEW button. Perform a quick release.

Zucchini Stew

(Prep + Cook Time: 20 minutes / Servings: 4)

Nutritional Info per Serving:

Calories 127, Protein 3, Carbs 16, Fat 6

Ingredients:

4 zucchinis, peeled and sliced
2 red bell peppers
1 eggplant, peeled and sliced

2 tbsp of olive oil
½ cup tomato juice
1 tsp of Italian seasoning

Directions:

1. Grease the bottom of the stainless steel insert with 2 tbsp. of olive oil.

2. Add zucchini, eggplant, peppers, tomato juice, Italian seasoning, salt, and half cup of water, stir well.

3. Press MANUAL and cook on HIGH pressure for 15 minutes. Serve chilled.

Chickpeas Stew

(Prep + Cook Time: 35 minutes / Servings: 4)

Nutritional Info per Serving:

Calories 363, Protein 22.3, Carbs 53.3, Fat 18.2

Ingredients:

1 lb. chickpeas, soaked
2 tomatoes, diced
2 oz. parsley, chopped
2 cups vegetable broth
2 onions, sliced

1 tbsp cayenne pepper
2 tbsp butter
1 tbsp olive oil
½ tsp salt and black pepper

Directions:

1. Heat oil on SAUTÉ mode and add onions. Stir fry for 3-4 minutes.

2. Add all ingredients, close the lid and set the steam release handle.

3. Press STEW and cook for 30 minutes.

4. Perform a quick release.

Chickpea Stew with Rice and Orange Juice

(Prep + Cook Time: 35 minutes / Servings: 6)

Nutritional Info per Serving:

Calories 268, Protein 9, Carbs 35, Fat 8

Ingredients:

1 lb. sweet potatoes, peeled and diced
4 cups vegetable broth
2 cans chickpeas, cooked
1 tbsp. olive oil
8 oz. orange juice
2 onions, sliced

6 oz. basmati rice
4 cups veggie broth
2 tsp. cumin
Salt and black pepper, to taste

Directions:

1. Set the Instant Pot to SAUTÉ.
2. Add the onions, and cook for 10 minutes.
3. Place all of the remaining ingredients, and stir to combine.
4. Select MANUAL and close the lid. Cook on HIGH for 5 minutes.
5. Release the pressure naturally. Serve and enjoy!

Beef Brisket Stew

(Prep + Cook Time: 95 minutes / Servings: 4)

Nutritional Info per Serving:

Calories 556, Protein 56, Carbs 40, Fat 18

Ingredients:

1 ½ lb. beef brisket, sliced
2 tbsp. oil
1 tbsp. flour
3 garlic cloves, minced
3 potatoes, cubed
1 onion, diced

2 carrots, peeled and chopped
2 celery stalks, chopped
1 tsp. Worcestershire sauce
2 cups beef stock
3 tbsp. tomato paste
1 tbsp. soy sauce

Directions:

1. Set your Instant Pot to SAUTÉ.
2. Heat the oil, and sauté the onions for 3 minutes.
3. Add garlic, and cook for 1 minute.
4. Add beef, and cook for 5 minutes per side.
5. Add carrots and celery, and cook for 2 minutes.
6. Stir in the remaining ingredients. Close the lid and select MANUAL.
7. Cook on HIGH for 70 minutes.
8. Release the pressure naturally. Serve and enjoy!

Rice and Risotto

Basic Instant White Rice

(Prep + Cook Time: 15 minutes / Servings: 4)

Nutritional Info per Serving:

Calories 225, Protein 4, Carbs 48, Fat 0.5

Ingredients:

1 cup white basmati rice

1 ½ cups water

Salt and black pepper, to taste

Directions:

1. Combine the water and rice in your Instant Pot.
2. Season with some salt and pepper.
3. Close the lid, select MANUAL, and cook on LOW for 8 minutes.
4. Release the pressure quickly.
5. Fluff the rice with a fork.
6. Serve and enjoy!

Simple Turmeric Brown Rice

(Prep + Cook Time: 30 minutes / Servings: 6)

Nutritional Info per Serving:

Calories 245, Protein 6.8, Carbs 49, Fat 2.3

Ingredients:

¼ tsp. garlic powder

1 tsp. turmeric

¼ tsp. black pepper

¾ tsp. sal

2 cups brown rice

2-½ - 3 cups vegetable stock

Directions:

1. Combine all of the ingredients in your Instant Pot.
2. Close the lid, select MANUAL, and cook on LOW for 22 minutes.
3. Do a quick pressure release.
4. Fluff the rice with a fork.
5. Serve and enjoy!

Garlic Rice with Black Beans

(Prep + Cook Time: 55 minutes / Servings: 4)

Nutritional Info per Serving:

Calories 690, Protein 28, Carbs 120, Fat 4

Ingredients:

1 onion, diced

2 cups dry black beans

9 cups water

2 cups brown rice

4 garlic cloves, minced

Juice of ½ lime

Directions:

1. Place all of the ingredients, except the lime, into your Instant Pot.
2. Stir to combine well.
3. Close the lid, select MANUAL, and cook for 30 minutes.
4. Release the pressure naturally, about 20 minutes.
5. Serve drizzled with lime juice.

Low-Carb Rice

(Prep + Cook Time: 25 minutes / Servings: 4)

Nutritional Info per Serving:

Calories 25, Protein 2, Carbs 5, Fat 0.1

Ingredients:

1 cauliflower rice
1 ½ cups water
2 tbsp. olive oil
¼ tsp. cumin
¼ tsp. turmeric
¼ tsp. garlic powder
Salt and black pepper, to taste

Directions:

1. Place the cauliflower florets in the steaming basket, and pour the water into the Instant Pot.
2. Close the lid, select STEAM, and cook for 2 minutes.
3. Release the pressure quickly.
4. Transfer to a plate, and discard the water.
5. Set the Instant Pot to SAUTÉ. Heat the oil.
6. Add cauliflower and spices. Mash with a fork, and let cook for 1 minute.
7. Serve and enjoy!

Risotto with Chicken and Vegetables

(Prep + Cook Time: 55 minutes / Servings: 4)

Nutritional Info per Serving:

Calories 520, Protein 31.6, Carbs 62, Fat 15.3

Ingredients:

½ lb. oz. chicken breasts, boneless, skinless, cut into pieces
6 oz. button mushrooms, sliced
6 oz. cauliflower, into small florets
1 cup rice
1 red, green, yellow bell peppers half-inch sliced
4 ears baby corn
5 cups water
2 carrots, chopped
½ cup sweet corn
2 tbsp. olive oil
1 tbsp. butter
½ tsp. freshly ground black pepper
1 tsp. fresh rosemary, finely chopped

Directions:

1. Pour in 3 cups of water and add the rice and butter.
2. Press RICE and cook until the end signal.
3. Perform a quick pressure release.
4. Remove the rice, and set aside.
5. Remove the stems from the mushrooms, and slice them.
6. Grease the stainless steel insert with 2 tbsp. of oil. Add the carrots and the cauliflower. Press SAUTÉ and cook for 15 minutes.
7. Add corn, baby corn, and bell peppers. Continue to cook for 5 minutes, stirring constantly.
8. Finally, add the mushrooms, stir and cook for 4-5 more minutes.
9. Press CANCEL, and remove the vegetables.
10. Combine them with rice and set aside.
11. Place the chicken in your Instant Pot, and pour in 2 cups of water.
12. Press MEAT button and cook for 8 minutes.
13. Press CANCEL and allow for a natural pressure release.
14. Add the rice and the vegetables, stir well and press the WARM (Keep Warm) button.

Instant Fried Rice with Peas

(Prep + Cook Time: 15 minutes / Servings: 4)

Nutritional Info per Serving:

Calories 250, Protein 7, Carbs 44, Fat 4.5

Ingredients:

1 tbsp. butter
1 onion, diced
1 egg
¼ cup soy sauce

1 ½ cups chicken stock
½ cup peas
1 cup basmati rice
2 garlic cloves, minced

Directions:

1. Set the Instant Pot to SAUTÉ.
2. Melt the butter.
3. Add onions, and cook for 2 minutes.
4. Add garlic, and cook 1 minute.
5. Scramble the egg, add to pot, and cook for an additional minute.
6. Stir in soy sauce, broth, and rice.
7. Close the lid, select RICE, and cook for 10 minutes.
8. Release the pressure quickly, and stir in the peas.
9. Select SAUTÉ, and cook for 1 minute.
10. Serve and enjoy!

Sweet Rice in Coconut Milk

(Prep + Cook Time: 30 minutes / Servings: 4)

Nutritional Info per Serving:

Calories 250, Protein 3, Carbs 45, Fat 7

Ingredients:

1 ½ cups water

1 cup sweet rice

2 tbsp. sugar

Pinch of salt

½ can coconut milk

Directions:

1. Combine the water and rice in the Instant Pot, and close the lid.
2. Select MANUAL, and cook on HIGH for 3 minutes.
3. Do a natural pressure release for 10 minutes.
4. Stir in the remaining ingredients.
5. Close the lid, and let rest for 10 minutes.
6. Serve and enjoy!

Sesame Risotto

(Prep + Cook Time: 35 minutes / Servings: 4)

Nutritional Info per Serving:

Calories 463, Protein 31.3, Carbs 46.7, Fat 18.6

Ingredients:

12 oz. lamb, half-inch thick pieces
1 cup rice
3 cups beef broth
½ cup green peas

4 tbsp. sesame seeds
½ tsp. thyme, dried
1 tsp. salt

Directions:

1. Place the meat in the Instant Pot and add beef broth.

2. Press MEAT and cook for 15 minutes. Perform a quick steam release.

3. Remove the meat from the Pot, keep the liquid.

4. Add the rice and green peas. Season with salt and thyme. Stir well and add the meat.

5. Press RICE button. When done, perform a quick release.

6. Sprinkle with sesame seeds and serve.

French Onion Brown Rice

(Prep + Cook Time: 35 minutes / Servings: 4)

Nutritional Info per Serving:

Calories 590, Protein 9.5, Carbs 75, Fat 26

Ingredients:

1 ¼ cups veggie stock
1 ¼ cups French onion soup, condensed

2 cups brown rice
½ cup butter

Directions:

1. Combine all of the ingredients in your Instant Pot.
2. Close the lid, and select MANUAL cooking mode.
3. Cook on HIGH for 22 minutes. Release the pressure naturally.
4. Serve and enjoy!

Buttery Spinach and Dill Basmati Rice

(Prep + Cook Time: 40 minutes / Servings: 6)

Nutritional Info per Serving:

Calories 213, Protein 6, Carbs 17, Fat 17

Ingredients:

1 cup spinach
3 oz. butter
1 tbsp. minced garlic
1 tsp. oregano
2 cups basmati rice

1 tbsp. salt
1 cup dill
4 cups broth
1 tsp. olive oil

Directions:

1. Set your Instant Pot to SAUTÉ.
2. Heat the oil and add garlic, butter, and rice. Cook for 5 minutes.
3. Stir in remaining ingredients.
4. Close the lid, select the RICE mode, and cook for 20 minutes.

Fruity Wild Rice with Almonds

(Prep + Cook Time: 35 minutes / Servings: 6)

Nutritional Info per Serving:

Calories 226, Protein 6, Carbs 43, Fat 3

Ingredients:

1 cup dried fruit
2 apples, peeled and chopped
1 pear, peeled and chopped
½ cup slivered almonds
3 ½ cups water

1 tsp. oil
1 tsp. cinnamon
2 tbsp. apple juice
1 tbsp. maple syrup
1 ½ cups wild rice

Directions:

1. Combine the water and rice in your Instant Pot, and close the lid.
2. Select MANUAL, and cook on HIGH pressure for 30 minutes.
3. Meanwhile, soak the dried fruit in the apple juice. Drain and chop it.
4. Release the pressure quickly. Place everything in the Instant Pot, and set it to SAUTÉ. Cook for 2 minutes and serve.

Mexican Chili Rice Casserole

(Prep + Cook Time: 35 minutes / Servings: 4)

Nutritional Info per Serving:

Calories 322, Protein 6, Carbs 63, Fat 2

Ingredients:

1 cup black beans, soaked
5 cups water
2 tsp. chili powder
2 tsp. onion powder

6 oz. tomato paste
2 cups brown rice
1 tsp. minced garlic

Directions:

1. Place all of the ingredients in your Instant Pot.
2. Stir to combine. Select MANUAL, and cook on HIGH for 28 minutes.
3. Release the pressure quickly.
4. Serve and enjoy!

Black Seafood Risotto

(Prep + Cook Time: 10 minutes / Servings: 8) 4

Nutritional Info per Serving:

Calories 323, Protein 20.1, Total Carbs 43.1 Fat 8.1

Ingredients:

1 lb. frozen seafood mix
1 cup brown rice
1 tbsp. calamari ink
2 garlic cloves, crushed

2 tbsp. rosemary, chopped
3 cups fish stock (or water)
olive oil for greasing

Directions:

1. Grease the bottom with oil and add all the ingredients.
2. Pour in 3 cups of stock and close the lid.
3. Set the steam release handle and press the RICE button.
4. Allow for a natural release.

Mushroom and Spinach Risotto

(Prep + Cook Time: 25 minutes / Servings: 4)

Nutritional Info per Serving:

Calories 320, Protein 10, Carbs 45, Fat 8

Ingredients:

½ cup onion, chopped
3 cups veggie broth
4 oz. mushrooms, chopped
3 garlic cloves, minced
¼ cup lemon juice
1 tsp. thyme
2 cups spinach

½ cup white wine
1 tbsp. oil
1 tbsp. butter
1 cup arborio rice
1 ½ tbsp. nutritional yeast

Directions:

1. Set your Instant Pot to SAUTÉ.
2. Heat the oil, and cook the onions and garlic for 3 minutes.
3. Add mushrooms, thyme, rice, wine, and broth, and close the lid.
4. Cook on HIGH on MANUAL for 5 minutes.
5. Release the pressure quickly.
6. Stir in spinach, butter, and yeast.
7. Serve and enjoy!

Simple Risotto

(Prep + Cook Time: 30 minutes / Servings: 6)

Nutritional Info per Serving:

Calories 266, Protein 7.8, Carbs 46, Fat 5

Ingredients:

1 onion, chopped
3 tbsp. grated Parmesan cheese
28 oz. chicken stock

1 ½ tbsp. oil
12 oz. arborio rice

Directions:

1. Set your Instant Pot to SAUTÉ.
2. Heat the oil, and cook the onion for 3 minutes.
3. Add rice and stock.
4. Close the lid, and cook on RICE mode, for 15 minutes.
5. Release the pressure naturally.
6. Stir in Parmesan cheese.
7. Serve and enjoy!

Marinated Smelt Risotto

(Prep + Cook Time: 30 minutes / Servings: 4)

Nutritional Info per Serving:

Calories 564, Protein 34.5, Carbs 27.1, Fat 42.5

Ingredients:

1 lb. fresh smelts, cleaned, heads removed
½ cup of rice
1 cup olive oil
¼ cup green peas, soaked overnight
5 oz. cherry tomatoes, halved
5 oz. okra
1 carrot, sliced

3 tbsp. vegetable oil
2 cups fish stock
¼ cup lemon juice
¼ cup orange juice
1 tsp. Dijon mustard
1 tsp. rosemary, chopped
2 garlic cloves, crushed
sea salt

Directions:

1. In a bowl, combine olive oil, lemon juice, orange juice, mustard, garlic, salt and rosemary.
2. Stir well and douse the fish in the mixture.
3. Refrigerate for one hour.
4. Meanwhile, press the SAUTÉ button on your Instant Pot and grease it with vegetable oil. Add carrot, cherry tomatoes, peas and okra.
5. Simmer for 12 minutes; then press CANCEL.
6. Add rice and fish stock. Press RICE and cook for 10 minutes.
7. Perform a quick release.
8. Add the fish to the Pot along with about half of the marinade.
9. Close the lid and press FISH button; cook for 5 minutes.
10. Allow for a natural pressure release.
11. Serve immediately.
12. Drizzle with the remaining marinade (optional).

Edamame Arborio Risotto

(Prep + Cook Time: 30 minutes / Servings: 4)

Nutritional Info per Serving:

Calories 356, Protein 7, Carbs 54, Fat 10

Ingredients:

1 tbsp. butter
1 tbsp. oil
½ cup white wine
1 cup edamame, thawed

2 tbsp. butter
4 cups chicken stock
1 onion, chopped
2 cups arborio rice

Directions:

1. Set your Instant Pot to SAUTÉ.
2. Heat the oil, and cook the onion for 3 minutes.
3. Add rice, and cook for 4 minutes.
4. Add wine, and cook until the rice absorbs it.
5. Pour the broth in, and close the lid.
6. Select MANUAL, and cook on HIGH for 8 minutes.
7. Stir in butter and edamame.
8. Serve and enjoy!

Veggie Risotto

(Prep + Cook Time: 30 minutes / Servings: 4)

Nutritional Info per Serving:

Calories 300, Protein 5, Carbs 48, Fat 4

Ingredients:

2 cups arborio rice
3 cups chicken stock

¼ cup heavy cream
1 carrot, peeled and shredded

½ onion, chopped
1 garlic clove, chopped
1 bell pepper, diced
5 oz. mushrooms, sliced

2 tbsp. butter
1 tbsp. olive oil
3 tbsp. Parmesan cheese

Directions:

1. Set your Instant Pot to SAUTÉ.
2. Heat the olive oil, and cook the onions and bell peppers for 3 minutes.
3. Add garlic, and cook for 1 minute.
4. Add mushrooms and carrots, and cook for 4 minutes.
5. Stir in broth, heavy cream, and rice.
6. Close the lid, select MANUAL, and cook for 12 minutes on HIGH.
7. Release the pressure quickly.
8. Stir in Parmesan and butter. Serve and enjoy!

Seafood Risotto

(Prep + Cook Time: 25 minutes / Servings: 4)

Nutritional Info per Serving:

Calories 325, Protein 12.7, Carbs 38.3 Fat 11.1

Ingredients:

1 cup rice
4 anchovies
5 oz. mussels
3 tbsp. olive oil
1 onion, chopped

1 garlic clove, crushed
1 oz. capers
1 tbsp. dried rosemary, chopped
1 tsp. ground chili pepper
salt

Directions:

1. Place the rice in your Instant Pot and add 2 and half cups of water.
2. Seal the lid and press RICE.

3. Perform a quick release and remove the rice.

4. Grease the bottom of the Instant Pot with oil, and SAUTÉ garlic and onions. Stirring constantly for 3 minutes.

5. Add mussels and rosemary. and continue to cook for 8 minutes.

6. Then, stir in the rice and season with salt and chili pepper.

7. Serve with anchovies and capers.

Shrimp Risotto

(Prep + Cook Time: 20 minutes / Servings: 4)

Nutritional Info per Serving:

Calories 470, Protein 24, Carbs 55, Fat 15.4

Ingredients:

1 ½ cups arborio rice

1 lb. shrimp, peeled and deveined

2 tbsp. white wine

1 onion, chopped

4 tbsp. butter, divided

¼ cup fresh herbs

¾ cup Parmesan cheese

2 garlic cloves, minced

4 ½ cups chicken broth

Directions

1. Set your Instant Pot to SAUTÉ.

2. Melt half of the butter, and cook the onion for 3 minutes.

3. Add garlic, and cook 1 minute.

4. Add rice and wine, and cook for 3 minutes.

5. Stir in the remaining ingredients, except remaining butter and cheese.

6. Close the lid, select MANUAL, and cook on HIGH for 5 minutes.

7. Release the pressure naturally.

8. Stir in Parmesan and butter.

9. Serve and enjoy!

Pasta

Garlic Beef and Onion Spaghetti

(Prep + Cook Time: 20 minutes / Servings: 4)

Nutritional Info per Serving:

Calories 600, Protein 72, Carbs 20, Fat 30

Ingredients:

1 lb. beef, chopped into small pieces
8 oz. spaghetti, uncooked
1 onion, chopped
2 garlic cloves, minced

2 tbsp. oil
1 ½ cups broth
Salt and black pepper, to taste

Directions:

1. Set your Instant Pot to SAUTÉ.
2. Heat the olive oil. Add the onion, and cook for 3 minutes.
3. Add garlic, and cook for 1 minute.
4. Add beef, and cook until browned.
5. Add the pasta and broth, and season with salt and pepper.
6. Close the lid, and cook on HIGH for 10 minutes.
7. Release the pressure quickly.
8. Serve and enjoy!

Chicken Pasta with Cherry Tomatoes

(Prep + Cook Time: 25 minutes / Servings: 6)

Nutritional Info per Serving:

Calories 425, Protein 25, Carbs 75, Fat 14

Ingredients:

1 onion, chopped
4 chicken breasts, diced
1 box linguine
1 cup water
5 garlic cloves, minced

30 cherry tomatoes, halved
1 cup breadcrumbs
1 tbsp. butter
½ tsp. oregano
1 jar spaghetti sauce

Directions:

1. Combine half of the spaghetti sauce, water, pasta, and chicken, in your Instant Pot.

2. Stir in garlic, oregano, and tomatoes.

3. Close the lid, select MANUAL, and cook on HIGH for 20 minutes.

4. Stir in butter and breadcrumbs.

5. Top with the remaining sauce (optional).

Cannelloni with Spinach and Mushrooms

(Prep + Cook Time: 35 minutes / Servings: 4)

Nutritional Info per Serving:

Calories 436, Protein 13, Carbs 41.6, Fat 25.3

Ingredients:

1 pack of 8.8 oz cannelloni
12 oz. spinach, torn
6 oz. button mushrooms, sliced
3 oz. ricotta cheese

2 oz. butter
1 cup of sour cream
½ cup milk
baking sheet

Directions:

1. Press SAUTÉ, melt the butter and add the mushrooms. Stir well and cook until soft.

2. Add spinach and milk. Cook for 5 more minutes, stirring constantly.

3. Add the cheese and stir.

4. Then press CANCEL.

5. Preheat the oven to 400 degrees F and line parchment paper over a baking sheet.

6. Fill the cannelloni with the spinach mixture and place them on the baking sheet. Bake for 18 minutes.

7. Remove from the oven and top with sour cream.

Mac and Cheese Variation 1

(Prep + Cook Time: 15 minutes / Servings: 4)

Nutritional Info per Serving:

Calories 487, Protein 15.1, Carbs 69.3, Fat 18.3

Ingredients:

1 lb. macaroni
2 oz. goat cheese, crumbled
1 tsp Dijon mustard
4 cups of water
½ cup skim milk

1 tsp oregano, dried
1 tbsp vegetable oil
1 tsp sea salt
1 tsp Italian seasoning mix
2 tbsp extra virgin olive oil

Directions:

1. Pour 4 cups of water, and add the macaroni and vegetable oil.

2. Set to MANUAL and cook for 3 minutes.

3. Perform a quick release.

4. Drain the macaroni in a large colander and set aside.

5. Press SAUTÉ, and add olive oil, dijon mustard, milk, oregano, Italian seasoning mix, and salt.

6. Cook for 6 minutes, stirring constantly.

7. Add macaroni and stir. Cook for 3 more minutes.

8. Remove from the pot and top with fresh goat's cheese

Bean and Beef Pasta in Beer Sauce

(Prep + Cook Time: 20 minutes / Servings: 4)

Nutritional Info per Serving:

Calories 630, Protein 44, Carbs 88, Fat 14

Ingredients:

1 lb. ground beef
2 cups corn kernels
8 oz. pasta
1 bell pepper, chopped
2 tbsp. sweet paprika
15 oz. can kidney beans, drained
12 oz. ale

1 onion, chopped
1 tbsp. olive oil
1 tbsp. minced garlic
1 tsp. cumin
28 oz. can diced tomatoes
Salt and black pepper, to taste

Directions:

1. Set your Instant Pot to SAUTÉ. Heat the oil, and cook the beef until browned.
2. Add onions and garlic, and cook for 3 minutes. Stir in the remaining ingredient.
3. Close the lid, and select MANUAL.
4. Cook on HIGH for 8 minutes.
5. Release the pressure quickly.

Bolognese Pasta

(Prep + Cook Time: 15 minutes / Servings: 4)

Nutritional Info per Serving:

Calories 590, Protein 47, Carbs 58, Fat 17

Ingredients:

1 ½ lb. ground beef
12 oz. water
24 oz. pasta sauce

8 oz. pasta
1 tsp. Italian seasoning

176

Directions:

1. Set your Instant Pot to SAUTÉ.
2. Coat the Instant Pot with cooking spray.
3. Add beef, and cook until browned.
4. Stir in the remaining ingredients.
5. Close the lid, select MANUAL, and cook on HIGH for 5 minutes.
6. Do a quick pressure release.
7. Serve and enjoy!

Tagliatelle with Mushrooms

(Prep + Cook Time: 20 minutes / Servings: 4)

Nutritional Info per Serving:

Calories 418, Protein 21.3, Carbs 53.1, Fat 17.1

Ingredients:

1 lb. tagliatelle
6 oz frozen mixed mushrooms
⅓ cup feta cheese
⅓ cup grated parmesan cheese

⅓ cup cooking cream
2 tbsp butter, unsalted
1 garlic cloves, crushed
1 tbsp Italian seasoning mix

Directions:

1. Press SAUTÉ, melt the butter and add garlic. Fry for 2 minutes, stirring continuously.
2. Add feta, parmesan, and cooking cream. Stir and cook for 3 more minutes.
3. Add the mushrooms and cook for another 6 minutes.
4. Press Cancel.
5. Add the tagliatelle and 1 cup of water.
6. Press MANUAL and set the timer to 5 minutes.
7. Allow for a natural pressure release.

Spaghetti with Shiitake and Veggies

(Prep + Cook Time: 15 minutes / Servings: 3)

Nutritional Info per Serving:

Calories 218, Protein 7.3, Carbs 32.4, Fat 10.6

Ingredients:

6 oz spaghetti

6 oz shiitake mushrooms, sliced

6 oz zucchini, sliced into strips

6 oz finely chopped leek

3 oz fresh baby spinach, chopped

1 garlic clove, crushed

1 carrot, sliced into strips

2 tbsp of oil

1 tbsp of soy sauce

1 tsp of ground ginger

Directions:

1. Grease the bottom of the Instant Pot with oil.

2. Press SAUTÉ and add carrot and garlic. Fry for 3 minutes.

3. Add the remaining ingredients and pour in 2 cups of water.

4. Seal the lid and press MANUAL for 4 minutes.

5. Release the pressure naturally.

Cheese Stuffed Rigatoni in a Meat Sauce

(Prep + Cook Time: 45 minutes / Servings: 6)

Nutritional Info per Serving:

Calories 600, Protein 40, Carbs 80, Fat 30

Ingredients:

1 lb. ground beef

16 oz. mozzarella cheese, grated

16 oz. ricotta cheese

2 eggs, whisked

1 tbsp. chopped parsley

1 tbsp. garlic powder

1 lb. cooked rigatoni

32 oz. marinara sauce

Directions:

1. Set your Instant Pot to SAUTÉ.
2. Coat the Instant Pot with cooking spray, and add the ground beef.
3. Sprinkle with garlic powder, and cook until browned.
4. Stir in marinara, and cook for 2 minutes.
5. Coat a baking pan with cooking spray, and transfer the sauce to the dish.
6. Place the rigatoni in a standing position.
7. Combine the cheeses, eggs, and parsley, in a bowl.
8. Spoon this mixture to a plastic bag, and cut off the tip.
9. Stuff the rigatoni with the cheese mixture.
10. Pour water into your Instant Pot.
11. Place the baking dish inside.
12. Close the lid, and set to MANUAL.
13. Cook on HIGH for 20 minutes.
14. Release the pressure naturally.
15. Serve and enjoy!

Beef and Tomato Sauce Macaroni

(Prep + Cook Time: 35 minutes / Servings: 4)

Nutritional Info per Serving:

Calories 523, Protein 26.1, Carbs 78.1, Fat 14.3

Ingredients:

1 pack macaroni, 16 oz.
5-6 oz. beef, braising steak cut into chunks
1 onion, chopped
1 tomato, diced
1 tbsp. tomato paste

2 tbsp. butter
1 tsp. cayenne pepper
1 bay leaf
1 tbsp. vegetable oil
salt and black pepper

Directions:

1. Grease the bottom of the Instant Pot with oil.
2. Select SAUTÉ and add the onion. Fry until translucent, stirring constantly.
3. Add butter, tomato, tomato paste, salt, black and cayenne pepper.
4. Cook until the tomato softens, stirring occasionally.
5. Add the beef chunks and 1 cup of water. Stir and close the lid.
6. Cook for 15 minutes on MEAT mode.
7. Perform a quick release and remove the meat; set aside.
8. Place the macaroni in the steel insert and add 2 cups of water.
9. Press MANUAL to 5 minutes. Perform a quick release.
10. Transfer the macaroni to a large bowl and pour in the beef sauce.
11. Serve and enjoy.

Hamburger Macaroni

(Prep + Cook Time: 20 minutes / Servings: 4)

Nutritional Info per Serving:

Calories 700, Protein 43, Carbs 46, Fat 35

Ingredients:

½ lb. ground beef
1 cup beef broth
2 oz. American cheese, shredded
4 oz. heavy cream

½ tbsp. garlic powder
½ tbsp. onion powder
8 oz. elbow macaroni
8 oz. cheddar cheese, grated

Directions:

1. Set your Instant Pot to SAUTÉ.
2. Coat it with cooking spray, and add the beef.
3. Add the spices, and cook until the beef is browned.
4. Stir in the remaining ingredients.

5. Close the lid, and select MANUAL.
6. Cook on HIGH for 4 minutes.
7. Release the pressure naturally.
8. Serve and enjoy!

Pasta with Fish Fillets

(Prep + Cook Time: 40 minutes / Servings: 4)

Nutritional Info per Serving:

Calories 414, Protein 23.1, Carbs 49.1, Fat 17.3

Ingredients:

1 lb. squid ink pasta
6 oz. trout fillet
1 cup olive oil
juice from 1 lemon

1 tsp. fresh rosemary, chopped
1 garlic cloves, crushed and halved
2 tbsp. fresh parsley, chopped
salt

Directions:

1. In a large bowl, combine olive oil, lemon juice, 1 garlic cloves, rosemary and 1 tsp. of salt. Stir well.
2. Add in the fillets in this mixture and refrigerate for half hour.
3. Remove the fillets from the fridge and add to Instant Pot along with 1 cup of water.
4. Close the lid, set the steam release handle and cook on MANUAL for 5 minutes.
5. Perform a quick pressure release and add the squid ink pasta, and another cup of water.
6. Close the lid, set the steam release handle and cook on MANUAL for 5 minutes.
7. Allow for a natural release. Sprinkle with parsley and serve.

Seafood Pasta

(Prep + Cook Time: 25 minutes / Servings: 4)

Nutritional Info per Serving:

Calories 265, Protein 25.8, Carbs 23.9, Fat 12.5

Ingredients:

1 lb. squid ink pasta, cooked
1 lb. fresh seafood mix
¼ cup olive oil
3 garlic cloves, crushed

1 tbsp. fresh parsley, chopped
1 tbsp. fresh rosemary, chopped
½ cup white wine
salt

Directions:

1. Grease the bottom of the Instant Pot with 3 tbsp. olive oil.

2. Press SAUTÉ and add garlic. Stir-fry for 3 minutes.

3. Add seafood mix, parsley, rosemary, olive oil, wine, half cup of water and a pinch of salt. Stir well.

4. Close the lid and set the steam release handle.

5. Press MANUAL and set 5 minutes.

6. Perform a quick release and open the lid to add the cooked pasta.

7. Stir and serve.

Alfredo and Chicken Fettuccine

(Prep + Cook Time: 10 minutes / Servings: 4)

Nutritional Info per Serving:

Calories 490, Protein 27, Carbs 59, Fat 16

Ingredients:

1 cup shredded chicken, cooked
8 oz. fettuccine

2 cups water
15 oz. Alfredo sauce

Directions:

1. Add pasta, chicken, and water in your Instant Pot.
2. Close the lid, select MANUAL, and cook on HIGH for 3 minutes.
3. Release the pressure quickly. Stir in the sauce.

Onion and Beef Cheesy Pasta

(Prep + Cook Time: 30 minutes / Servings: 4)

Nutritional Info per Serving:

Calories 462, Protein 35, Carbs 43, Fat 15

Ingredients:

½ lb. ground beef
1 ½ beef bouillon cubes
4 oz. cheddar cheese, grated

1 packet onion soup mix
¾ pound elbow macaroni
2 ½ cup water

Directions:

1. Set your Instant Pot to SAUTÉ. Add the beef, and cook until brown.
2. Stir in bouillon, onion soup mix, water, and macaroni.
3. Close the lid, and select MANUAL.
4. Cook on HIGH for 5 minutes.
5. Release the pressure naturally.
6. Stir in the cheddar cheese.
7. Serve and enjoy!

Spicy Mexican Beef Pasta

(Prep + Cook Time: 10 minutes / Servings: 4)

Nutritional Info per Serving:

Calories 425, Protein 25, Carbs 55, Fat 21

Ingredients:

½ lb. ground beef
1 ½ cups water
8 oz. can black beans
1 cup Doritos

8 oz. salsa
1 packet taco seasoning
8 oz. pasta
½ cup shredded cheddar

Directions:

1. Set the Instant Pot to SAUTÉ.
2. Coat with cooking spray.
3. Add beef and taco seasoning, and cook until browned.
4. Add pasta, beans, salsa, and water to the pot.
5. Close the lid, and select MANUAL.
6. Cook on HIGH for 4 minutes. Release the pressure naturally.
7. Arrange Dorito's in a baking dish.
8. Top with the pasta, and sprinkle the cheese over it.
9. Pour water into your Instant Pot, and place the dish inside.
10. Close the lid, and cook on HIGH for 5 minutes.
11. Serve and enjoy!

Creamy Bowtie Pasta with Shrimp

(Prep + Cook Time: 15 minutes / Servings: 4)

Nutritional Info per Serving:

Calories 511 Protein 33, Carbs 47, Fat 22

Ingredients:

8 oz. bowtie pasta
1 yellow onion, chopped
12 oz. frozen shrimp
1 tbsp. olive oil
½ cup heavy cream

1 cup grated Parmesan cheese
2 ½ cups chicken broth
1 garlic clove, minced
Salt and black pepper, to taste

Directions:

1. Set the Instant Pot to SAUTÉ. Heat the oil.
2. Cook the onion for 3 minutes.
3. Add garlic, and cook for 1 minute.
4. Stir in shrimp, pasta, broth, salt, and pepper.
5. Cook for 7 minutes.
6. Release the pressure quickly.
7. Drain the pasta and shrimp, and return them back to the pot.
8. Stir in Parmesan and cream, and cook on SAUTÉ for 2 minutes.
9. Serve and enjoy!

Tomato Pasta with Tuna and Capers

(Prep + Cook Time: 20 minutes / Servings: 4)

Nutritional Info per Serving:

Calories 54, Protein 3, Carbs 5, Fat 2

Ingredients:

30 oz. can diced tomatoes
2 garlic cloves, minced
3 tbsp. capers

2 cans of tuna, 5 oz. each
2 tbsp. olive oil
4 cups pasta, cooked

Directions:

1. Set the Instant Pot to SAUTÉ.
2. Heat the oil, and cook the garlic until fragrant.
3. Stir in the remaining ingredients.
4. Close the lid, and select MANUAL.
5. Cook on high for 1 minute.
6. Release the pressure naturally.
7. Serve and enjoy!

Mac and Cheese Variation 2

(Prep + Cook Time: 10 minutes / Servings: 4)

Nutritional Info per Serving:

Calories 650, Protein 30, Carbs 48, Fat 49

Ingredients:

2 cups chicken stock
½ cup milk
1 tbsp. butter
1 tsp. pepper

2 ½ cups elbow macaroni
1 cup heavy cream
1 ½ cup shredded pepper jack
1 tsp. salt

Directions:

1. Place all of the ingredients into your Instant Pot.
2. Stir to combine.
3. Close the lid, and select MANUAL.
4. Cook on HIGH for 7 minutes.
5. Release the pressure quickly.
6. Serve and enjoy!

Macaroni and Tuna Casserole

(Prep + Cook Time: 10 minutes / Servings: 4)

Nutritional Info per Serving:

Calories 700, Protein 40, Carbs 5, Fat 22

Ingredients:

1 ½ cups shredded cheddar cheese
2 cans cream of mushroom soup,
10.5 oz. each
4 cups macaroni

3 ½ cups water
2 cans tuna
1 cup peas, frozen
Salt and black pepper, to taste

Directions:

1. Combine everything in your Instant Pot, except the cheese.
2. Select MANUAL, and cook on HIGH for 4 minutes.
3. Release the pressure quickly.
4. Sprinkle the cheese over, and cook for 5 more minutes on HIGH.

Classic Lasagna from the Instant Pot

(Prep + Cook Time: 40 minutes / Servings: 6)

Nutritional Info per Serving:

Calories 400, Protein 25, Carbs 27, Fat 22

Ingredients:

1 lb. ground beef
32 oz. ricotta cheese
8 oz. lasagna noodles
5 oz. shredded mozzarella cheese
¼ cup water
1 onion, diced

1 tbsp. olive oil
24 oz. tomato sauce
2 eggs
1 garlic clove, minced
⅓ cup grated Parmesan cheese
1 tsp. Italian seasoning

Directions:

1. Set your Instant Pot to SAUTÉ.
2. Heat the olive oil, and add the onion, garlic, and beef.
3. Cook until the beef brownsAdd pasta sauce and water, stir well, and transfer entire mixture to a bowl.
4. In another bowl combine the ricotta, eggs, parmesan, and Italians seasoning.
5. Fill the Pot with ¼-inch water. Add ¼ of the beef mixture on the bottom.
6. Arrange ⅓ of the noodles. Spread ⅓ of the ricotta mixture, and some of the beef sauce. Repeat the layers until you use all mixture.
7. Top the final layer with mozzarella cheese. Close the lid, select MANUAL, and cook on HIGH for 7 minutes. Do a quick pressure release.

Turmeric Couscous

(Prep + Cook Time: 10 minutes / Servings: 4)

Nutritional Info per Serving:

Calories 201, Protein 7, Carbs 35, Fat 2.3

Ingredients:

8 oz. couscous

2 tbsp. butter

1 tsp. turmeric

1 ¼ cups chicken broth

Directions:

1. Set your Instant Pot to SAUTÉ.
2. Add the butter and turmeric, and cook just until the butter melts.
3. Add couscous and broth and stir to combine.
4. Close the lid, select MANUAL, and cook on HIGH for 5 minutes.
5. Release the pressure quickly.
6. Season with some salt and pepper.
7. Serve and enjoy!

Chicken Cordon Bleu Pasta

(Prep + Cook Time: 50 minutes / Servings: 4)

Nutritional Info per Serving:

Calories 600, Protein 44, Carbs 40, Fat 40

Ingredients:

½ cup breadcrumbs

½ lb. chicken breast, cut into strips

½ lb. ham, cubed

8 oz. Swiss cheese

1 cup chicken broth

1 tbsp. butter

4 oz. gouda cheese

8 oz. pasta

4 oz. heavy cream

Directions:

1. Combine pasta, broth, chicken, and ham in your Instant Pot.
2. Close the lid, and cook on HIGH for 25 minutes.
3. Release the pressure quickly.
4. Stir in the remaining ingredients, except the breadcrumbs.
5. Cook on SAUTÉ for 3 minutes. Sprinkle the breadcrumbs on top.

Gluten-Free Spaghetti

(Prep + Cook Time: 20 minutes / Servings: 4)

Nutritional Info per Serving:

Calories 178, Protein 1, Carbs 39, Fat 3

Ingredients:

1 whole spaghetti squash   2 cups water

Directions:

1. Cut the squash lengthwise. Discard the seeds.
2. Pour the water into the Instant Pot, and place the squash in the steaming basket.
3. Close the lid, and select MANUAL. Cook on HIGH for 6 minutes.
4. Release the pressure quickly.
5. With a fork, pull of the squash flesh, making spaghetti strings.
6. Serve as desired and enjoy!

Pizza Pasta

(Prep + Cook Time: 15 minutes / Servings: 6)

Nutritional Info per Serving:

Calories 454, Protein 20, Carbs 55, Fat 18

Ingredients:

1lb. sausage, sliced
8 oz. pizza sauce
16 oz. pasta sauce
1 pound pasta
1 tsp. Italian seasoning

8 oz. mozzarella cheese, shredded and divided
2 tsp. minced garlic
20 slices pepperoni, divided
1 tbsp. butter

Directions:

1. Melt the butter in the Instant Pot on SAUTÉ.

2. Add sausage and garlic, and cook for 5 minutes.

3. Stir in pizza sauce, pasta sauce, pasta, seasoning, half of the pepperoni, and half of the cheese.

4. Close the lid, and select MANUAL.

5. Cook on HIGH for 5 minutes.

6. Do a quick pressure release.

7. Stir in the remaining cheese and pepperoni.

8. Serve and enjoy!

Pasta Caprese

(Prep + Cook Time: minutes / Servings: 4)

Nutritional Info per Serving:

Calories 480, Protein 18, Carbs 80, Fat 9

Ingredients:

4 cups penne
1 onion, sliced
15 oz. tomato sauce
1 cup mozzarella balls
4 handful basil leaves, divided
6 garlic cloves, minced

2 cups water
1 cup halved grape tomatoes
1 tbsp. olive oil
¼ cup balsamic vinegar
1 tsp. salt

Directions:

1. Set your Instant Pot to SAUTÉ.
2. Heat the oil, and sauté garlic for a minute.
3. Stir in pasta sauce, half of the basil, tomatoes, pasta, water, and salt.
4. Close the lid, select MANUAL, and cook on HIGH for 4 minutes.
5. Release the pressure naturally. Add mozzarella and basil.
6. Serve and enjoy!

Roasted Veggies Pasta

(Prep + Cook Time: 25 minutes / Servings: 4)

Nutritional Info per Serving:

Calories 420, Protein 5, Carbs 57, Fat 8

Ingredients:

4 cups pasta
1 tomato, chopped
2 garlic cloves, minced
½ onion, chopped
1 bell pepper, chopped
1 zucchini, chopped

⅓ cups grated Parmesan cheese
3 cups chicken broth
½ cup heavy cream
Salt and black pepper
1 tbsp. oil

Directions:

1. Set your Instant Pot to SAUTÉ.
2. Heat the oil, and cook the onion and bell pepper for 3 minutes.
3. Add garlic, and cook for 1 minute.
4. Add zucchini and cook for 1 minute.
5. Stir in pasta, broth, and heavy cream, and season with salt and pepper.
6. Close the lid, select MANUAL, and cook on HIGH for 5 minutes.
7. Release the pressure naturally. Stir in the Parmesan cheese.

Chicken Florentine Pasta

(Prep + Cook Time: 20 minutes / Servings: 4)

Nutritional Info per Serving:

Calories 520, Protein 27, Carbs 60, Fat 12

Ingredients:

4 cups chicken broth

4 oz. mozzarella cheese, sliced

2 garlic cloves, minced

16 oz. spaghetti

2 cans mushroom soup

4 cups baby spinach

2 chicken breasts, chopped

Directions:

1. Set your Instant Pot to SAUTÉ.

2. Add chicken and broth, and bring it to a boil.

3. Stir in the remaining ingredients.

4. Close the lid, select MANUAL, and cook on HIGH for 4 minutes.

5. Serve and enjoy!

Fish and Seafood

Shrimp Creole

(Prep + Cook Time: 20 minutes / Servings: 4)

Nutritional Info per Serving:

Calories 264, Protein 31, Carbs 24, Fat 4.5

Ingredients:

1 lb. jumbo shrimp, peeled, deveined
2 celery stalks, diced
2 garlic cloves, minced
2 tsp. olive oil

1 tsp. thyme
1 onion, diced
28 oz. can tomatoes, diced
1 bell pepper, diced

Directions:

1. Set the Instant Pot to SAUTÉ. Heat the oil.

2. Add onions, garlic, and celery, and cook for 3 minutes.

3. Add the remaining ingredients. Stir to combine.

4. Close the lid and select MANUAL. Cook on HIGH for 1 minute.

5. Release the pressure quickly. Set it to SAUTÉ mode again, and cook until the liquid is reduced, at least 10 minutes.

Halibut Dijon

(Prep + Cook Time: 5 minutes / Servings: 4)

Nutritional Info per Serving:

Calories 191, Protein 41, Carbs 0.1, Fat 2

Ingredients:

1 tbsp. Dijon mustard

4 halibut fillets

Directions:

1. Pour 2 cups of water into your Instant Pot.
2. Brush the fish fillets with mustard.
3. Arrange the fish in the steaming basket.
4. Close the lid, and select MANUAL.
5. Cook on HIGH for 3 minutes.
6. Release the pressure quickly.
7. Serve and enjoy!

Quick Salmon and Broccoli

(Prep + Cook Time: 5 minutes / Servings: 4)

Nutritional Info per Serving:

Calories 119, Protein 16, Carbs 5, Fat 5

Ingredients:

10 oz. broccoli florets
4 salmon fillets
1 ½ cups water

1 tsp. garlic powder
Salt and pepper, to taste

Directions:

1. Season the salmon with garlic powder, salt, and pepper.
2. Sprinkle the broccoli with salt and pepper, as well.
3. Pour the water into your Instant Pot.
4. Arrange the salmon in the steaming basket and scatter the broccoli around the fillets.
5. Close the lid, and select MANUAL.
6. Cook on HIGH for 2 minutes.
7. Release the pressure quickly.

8. Serve and enjoy!

Alaskan Cod with Cherry Tomatoes

(Prep + Cook Time: 15 minutes / Servings: 4)

Nutritional Info per Serving:

Calories 400, Protein 40, Carbs 4, Fat 17

Ingredients:

2 cups cherry tomatoes

4 Alaskan cod fillets

2 tbsp. butter, melted

Salt and pepper, to taste

Directions:

1. Place the cherry tomatoes in a baking dish. Top with the cod fillets.
2. Drizzle the butter over the fish, and season with salt and pepper.
3. Place the dish in the Instant Pot. Close the lid, and select MANUAL.
4. Cook on HIGH for 5 minutes. Release the pressure naturally.

Lemon Chili Salmon

(Prep + Cook Time: 10 minutes / Servings: 4)

Nutritional Info per Serving:

Calories 182, Protein 25, Carbs 3, Fat 8

Ingredients:

1 lemon, sliced

2 tbsp. chipotle chili pepper

4 salmon fillets

Juice of 1 lemon

Directions:

1. Pour 2 cups of water into your Instant Pot.
2. Season the salmon with the lemon juice, salt and black pepper.

3. Top with chili pepper and lemon slices. Close the lid and select MANUAL.

4. Cook on high for 4 minutes. Release the pressure quickly.

Steamed Sea Bream

(Prep + Cook Time: 45 minutes / Servings: 4)

Nutritional Info per Serving:

Calories 421, Protein 35.3, Carbs 12.1 Fat 16.8

Ingredients:

2 pieces sea bream, cleaned
4 cups fish stock
4 tbsp. lemon juice
4 tbsp. olive oil

½ tbsp. garlic powder
1 tsp. rosemary sprigs
1 tsp. Italian seasoning
sea salt

Directions:

1. In a small bowl, combine olive oil, lemon juice, rosemary, Italian seasoning, sea salt and garlic powder.

2. Brush the fish and wrap tightly with plastic foil.

3. Refrigerate for 30 minutes before cooking.

4. Pour in the fish stock in your Instant Pot.

5. Adjust the steamer insert and place the fish.

6. Close, set the steam release handle and select FISH for 8 minutes.

7. Once ready, perform a quick release. Serve immediately.

Seafood Chickpeas

(Prep + Cook Time: 20 minutes / Servings: 5)

Nutritional Info per Serving:

Calories 258, Protein 27.1, Carbs 25.8, Fat 11.1

Ingredients:

1 lb. shrimp, cleaned and deveined

3 cups fish broth

1 cup scallions, chopped

1 carrot, chopped

1 cup chickpeas, soaked

½ tbsp. Italian seasoning

salt and black pepper

Directions:

1. Add all ingredients in the Instant Pot.

2. Close the lid and adjust the steam release handle.

3. Press MANUAL and cook on HIGH for 14 minutes.

4. When done, press CANCEL and release naturally.

5. Open the lid after 10 minutes and serve warm.

Garlic Sockeye Salmon

(Prep + Cook Time: 10 minutes / Servings: 4)

Nutritional Info per Serving:

Calories 194, Protein 24, Carbs 1, Fat 10

Ingredients:

1 ½ cups water

4 salmon fillets

1 tsp. Dijon mustard

1 tsp. garlic powder

1 garlic clove, minced

1 tbsp. lemon juice

Salt and black pepper, to taste

Directions:

1. Whisk together the lemon juice, mustard, garlic powder, and minced garlic.

2. Brush this mixture over the salmon.

3. Pour the water into your Instant Pot.

4. Arrange the salmon fillets on the rack.

5. Close the lid, and select MANUAL.

6. Cook on HIGH for 3 - 4 minutes.
7. Release the pressure quickly.

Cajun Shrimp and Asparagus

(Prep + Cook Time: 25 minutes / Servings: 4)

Nutritional Info per Serving:

Calories 329, Protein 56, Carbs 11, Fat 6

Ingredients:

1 tbsp. Cajun seasoning

1 lb. shrimp, peeled and deveined

1 tsp. olive oil

1 asparagus bunch, 12, trimmed

1 ½ cups water

Directions:

1. Pour the water into your Instant Pot.
2. Arrange the asparagus on the rack, in a single layer.
3. Place the shrimp on top.
4. Drizzle with olive oil, and season with Cajun seasoning.
5. Close the lid, and select the STEAM mode.
6. Cook on LOW for 2 minutes.
7. Release the pressure quickly.

Mackerel with Spinach and Potatoes

(Prep + Cook Time: 30 minutes / Servings: 4)

Nutritional Info per Serving:

Calories 267, Protein 14.5, Carbs 23.5, Fat 12.1

Ingredients:

4 medium-sized mackerels, skin on

1 lb. fresh spinach, torn

4 potatoes, peeled and sliced
¼ cup olive oil
2 garlic cloves, crushed

1 tbsp. rosemary, dried, chopped
2 springs fresh mint leaves, chopped
juice of 1 lemon

Directions:

1. Grease the bottom of the Instant Pot with 4 tbsp. of olive oil.
2. Press SAUTÉ button and add garlic and rosemary.
3. Stir-fry for a minute and add the spinach.
4. Sprinkle with salt and cook for 5 more minutes, stirring occasionally.
5. Remove the spinach from the cooker and set aside.
6. Add the remaining olive oil to the pot and make a lay in the potatoes.
7. Place the fish and drizzle with lemon juice and sea salt.
8. Pour in 1 cup of water and close the lid.
9. Adjust the steam release handle and press FISH. Cook for 8 minutes.
10. Release the steam naturally and transfer the fish and the potatoes to a serving plate. Serve with spinach.

Orange Salmon

(Prep + Cook Time: 15 minutes / Servings: 3)

Nutritional Info per Serving:

Calories 265, Protein 33.5, Carbs 21.5, Fat 21.3

Ingredients:

1 lb. salmon fillets
2 tbsp. cornstarch
1 cup squeeze orange juice
1 tsp. orange zest

1 tsp. Himalayan salt
½ tsp. black pepper, freshly ground
½ tsp. garlic, minced

Directions:

1. Grease the stainless steel insert with olive oil.

2. Add all the ingredients and close the lid.
3. Press MANUAL and cook on HIGH for 15 minutes.
4. Release the steam naturally.

Green Salmon

(Prep + Cook Time: 25 minutes / Servings: 4)

Nutritional Info per Serving:

Calories 451, Protein 41.1, Carbs 15.3, Fat 25.8

Ingredients:

1 lb. salmon filets, boneless
1 lb. fresh spinach, torn
3 tbsp. olive oil
1 garlic cloves, finely chopped

1 tbsp. lemon juice
1 tbsp. fresh rosemary, chopped
sea salt and black pepper

Directions:

1. Grease the bottom of the Instant Pot with 2 tbsp. olive oil.
2. Place the salmon filets and season with rosemary, salt and pepper.
3. Drizzle with lemon juice, add half cup of water and close.
4. Set the steam release handle and press the MANUAL button.
5. Cook on HIGH pressure for 4 minutes.
6. When done, press CANCEL and turn off the Instant Pot.
7. In a large pot, place the torn spinach and cover with water.
8. Bring to a boil and cook for 2 -3 minutes or until tender. Drain in a colander.
9. Remove the salmon from the Instant Pot and place the spinach at the bottom. Pour half cup of water and add garlic.
10. Top with salmon and press SAUTÉ and cook for 7 - 8 minutes more.

Marinated Salmon Fillet

(Prep + Cook Time: 55 minutes / Servings: 4)

Nutritional Info per Serving:

Calories 285, Protein 26.5, Carbs 13.1 Fat 22.3

Ingredients:

1 lb. fresh salmon fillets
2 cups fish stock
2 garlic cloves, crushed
¼ cup olive oil

juice of 1 lemon
1 tbsp. oregano leaves, chopped
¼ tbsp. red pepper flakes

Directions:

1. In a bowl, combine the olive oil, lemon juice, oregano, garlic, red pepper and a pinch of sea salt.
2. Brush the mixture over the fillets and cool for 30 minutes.
3. Pour in the fish stock in the Instant Pot.
4. Separate the fillets from the marinade and pat dry with paper towel.
5. Place the fillets on the steamer insert.
6. Close the lid.
7. Set the steam release handle and press FISH.
8. Once ready, perform a quick release.
9. Serve and enjoy!

Instant Shrimp Casserole with Tomatoes

(Prep + Cook Time: 30 minutes / Servings: 4)

Nutritional Info per Serving:

Calories 300, Protein 22, Carbs 17, Fat 16

Ingredients:

1 ½ lb. tomatoes, chopped
1 ½ lb. shrimp, peeled and deveined
¼ cup chopped cilantro
1 tbsp. lime juice
1 onion, chopped
2 tbsp. olive oil
1 jalapeño, diced
1 cup shredded cheddar cheese
½ cup clam juice
2 garlic cloves, minced

Directions:

1. Set your Instant Pot to SAUTÉ.
2. Heat the olive oil, and sauté the onion for 3 minutes.
3. Add garlic, and cook for 1 minute.
4. Stir in tomatoes, clam juice, and cilantro.
5. Close the lid and select MANUAL.
6. Cook on HIGH for 9 minutes.
7. Release the pressure naturally.
8. Stir in cilantro and shrimp, and cook on HIGH for 1 minute.
9. Stir in cheddar. Sprinkle with lemon juice.

Mahi-Mahi with Green Chilies

(Prep + Cook Time: 20 minutes / Servings: 4)

Nutritional Info per Serving:

Calories 325, Protein 14, Carbs 18, Fat 22

Ingredients:

4 mahi-mahi fillets
⅓ cups chopped green chilies
2 tbsp. butter, melted

Salt and black pepper, to taste
1 ½ cups water

Directions:

1. Brush the mahi-mahi with melted butter.
2. Sprinkle with salt and pepper.
3. Pour the water into your Instant Pot.
4. Arrange the fish fillets on the rack.
5. Top with the green chilies.
6. Close the lid and select MANUAL.
7. Cook on HIGH for 5 minutes. Release the pressure quickly and serve.

Red Pollock

(Prep + Cook Time: 45 minutes / Servings: 4)

Nutritional Info per Serving:

Calories 387, Protein 24.4, Carbs 12.3, Fat 24.1

Ingredients:

1 lb. pollock fillet
4 large tomatoes, peeled
4 garlic cloves, crushed
1 onion, chopped

2 cups fish stock
2 bay leaves, whole
½ cup olive oil
salt and black pepper

Directions:

1. Press SAUTÉ and heat 2 tbsp. olive oil.
2. Add onion and stir-fry until translucent. Add the tomatoes and cook until they soften. Keep adding fish stock from time to time.
3. Once the tomatoes have softened and the liquid has evaporated, add the remaining ingredients. Press CANCEL, close the lid and set the steam handle. Press STEW and cook for 16 minutes.

Grilled Catfish

(Prep + Cook Time: 65 minutes / Servings: 6)

Nutritional Info per Serving:

Calories 311, Protein 18.5, Carbs 11.1 Fat 19.5

Ingredients:

1 lb. of flathead catfish
3 oranges, sliced into ¼ - inch thick slices
3 cups fish stock
1 cup orange juice

½ cup lemon juice
½ cup olive oil
1 tbsp. dried rosemary
1 tsp. chili flakes
salt and black pepper

Directions:

1. Line the orange slices in your Instant Pot.
2. In a large bowl, combine the orange juice, lemon juice, olive oil, rosemary, chili flakes, black pepper and salt.
3. Brush the fish with this mixture and cool for 45 minutes.
4. Set the steamer insert of your Instant Pot.
5. Drain the fish and pour in the fish stock and the marinade, then place the fish onto the insert.
6. Close the lid, press MANUAL and cook for 20 minutes.

Caramelized Tilapia Fillets

(Prep + Cook Time: 55 minutes / Servings: 4)

Nutritional Info per Serving:

Calories 150, Protein 21, Carbs 18, Fat 2

Ingredients:

1 lb. tilapia fillets
1 scallion, minced
1 cup coconut water
3 garlic cloves, minced
⅓ cup water

3 tbsp. fish sauce
¼ cup sugar
Salt and black pepper, to taste
1 red chili, minced

Directions:

1. Marinate the tilapia in fish sauce, salt, pepper, and garlic for 30 minutes on the counter.
2. Combine the water and sugar in your Instant Pot.
3. Cook on SAUTÉ until caramelized.
4. Add the fish and coconut water in the Instant Pot.
5. Close the lid, and select MANUAL. Cook on HIGH for 10 minutes.
6. Top with spring onions and red chili.

Garlic Octopus in Lime Juice

(Prep + Cook Time: 20 minutes / Servings: 4)

Nutritional Info per Serving:

Calories 120, Protein 9, Carbs 3, Fat 3

Ingredients:

10 oz. octopus
3 tbsp. lime juice
2 tsp. garlic powder
1 ½ cups water

1 tsp. chopped cilantro
2 tbsp. olive oil
Salt and black pepper, to taste

Directions:

1. Place the octopus in your Instant Pot.
2. Sprinkle with olive oil, salt, pepper, and garlic powder.
3. Pour the water around it (not on it!).
4. Close the lid and select MANUAL. Cook on HIGH for 8 minutes.
5. Sprinkle lime juice over and cilantro.

Cheesy Haddock

(Prep + Cook Time: 35 minutes / Servings: 4)

Nutritional Info per Serving:

Calories 194, Protein 18, Carbs 6.5, Fat 18

Ingredients:

12 oz. haddock fillets
½ cup heavy cream
1 tsp. ground ginger

5 oz. cheddar cheese, grated
Salt and black pepper, to taste
1 tbsp. butter

Directions:

1. Combine the ginger, salt, and pepper, in a small bowl.

2. Rub the haddock with the spice mixture.

3. Melt the butter in the Instant Pot on SAUTÉ.

4. Add haddock, and cook on SAUTÉ for 2 minutes per side.

5. Pour the cream and cheese over the fillets.

6. Close the lid, select MANUAL, and cook on STEW for 10 minutes.

7. Release the pressure naturally.

Catfish with Dill and Soy

(Prep + Cook Time: 15 minutes / Servings: 4)

Nutritional Info per Serving:

Calories 103, Protein 11, Carbs 2.5, Fat 5

Ingredients:

1 tbsp. olive oil
2 tbsp. soy sauce
¼ cup water

2 tsp. chopped dill
4 catfish fillets
3 garlic cloves, minced

Directions:

1. Heat the oil in your Instant Pot on SAUTÉ.

2. Add garlic, and cook for 1 minute.

3. Add soy sauce and dill.

4. Add the catfish and season with salt and pepper.

5. Cook for about 4 minutes per side.

Cod in Maple Sauce

(Prep + Cook Time: 20 minutes / Servings: 3)

Nutritional Info per Serving:

Calories 468, Protein 32.1, Carbs 58.1, Fat 12.1

Ingredients:

1 lb. cod fillets, skinless and boneless
½ cup soy sauce
2 garlic cloves, chopped
1 cup maple syrup

butter
juice of 1 lemon
salt and black pepper
1 tsp. sea salt

Directions:

1. In a large mixing bowl, combine and stir soy sauce, garlic, maple syrup, lemon juice, salt and pepper. Set aside.
2. Grease the Instant Pot with 1 tbsp. butter. Place the fillets on the bottom and pour maple sauce over. Seal the lid and adjust the steam release handle.
3. Select FISH and cook for 9 minutes on HIGH pressure.
4. When ready, press CANCEL and release the steam naturally.

Collard Greens with Seafood

(Prep + Cook Time: 35 minutes / Servings: 4)

Nutritional Info per Serving:

Calories 355, Protein 41.1, Carbs 12.5, Fat 17.6

Ingredients:

1 lb. shrimp
6 oz. octopus, chopped into pieces
½ lb. collard greens, rinsed, drained and chopped
1 tomato, peeled and diced

2 cups fish stock
3 tbsp. extra virgin olive oil
2 garlic cloves
2 tbsp. fresh parsley, chopped

Directions:

1. Place the shrimp, octopus, tomato and fish stock in the Instant Pot.
2. Close the lid and adjust the steam release handle.
3. Press MANUAL and the timer to 15 minutes.

4. Once ready, open the lid and remove the shrimp and the octopus, and drain the liquid. Grease the bottom of the Pot with olive oil and press SAUTÉ.
5. Stir-fry garlic and add parsley and collard greens.
6. Let simmer for 12 minutes. Serve with shrimp and octopus.

Fish Fillets with Spinach

(Prep + Cook Time: 50 minutes / Servings: 4)

Nutritional Info per Serving:

Calories 465, Protein 41.5, Carbs 10.5, Fat 28.8

Ingredients:

1 lb. trout fillets
5 oz. fresh spinach, torn
3 tbsp. lemon juice
3 cups fish stock
¼ cup olive oil

3 garlic cloves, crushed
2 tomatoes, peeled and diced
1 tbsp. thyme, dried
½ tbsp. rosemary, fresh

Directions:

1. In a large bowl, combine the olive oil, thyme, rosemary, lemon juice. Stir well and submerge the fillets in the mixture. Cool for 45 minutes.
2. Remove from the fridge, drain the fillets and keep the marinade.
3. Grease the stainless steel cooking insert of the Instant Pot wit 1/4 cup of the marinade. Add the fillets, fish stock and seal the lid.
4. Set the steam release handle, press FISH button and cook for 10 minutes.
5. Perform a quick release, and open the lid. Remove the fish, and set aside.
6. Pour the remaining marinade into the Pot. Press SAUTÉ and add tomatoes.
7. Cook until the tomatoes soften; then remove.
8. Grease the bottom with olive oil, add garlic and spinach. Cook for 7 minutes, then press CANCEL.
9. Remove from the Pot and transfer to a plate. Add the fish and top with with tomato sauce.

Buttery Crab Legs

(Prep + Cook Time: 10 minutes / Servings: 4)

Nutritional Info per Serving:

Calories 300, Protein 40, Carbs 3, Fat 6

Ingredients:

⅓ cup butter

2 garlic cloves, minced

3 lb. crab legs

1 tsp. olive oil

Directions:

1. Pour 2 cups of water into your Instant Pot. Place the crab legs in the steaming basket. Close the lid, and select the STEAM mode.
2. Cook for 3 - 4 minutes. Transfer to a plate. Set the Instant Pot to SAUTÉ.
3. Add oil and butter, and heat until butter is melted. Add garlic, and cook for 1 minute. Pour garlic butter sauce over the crab legs.

Instant Crunchy Tuna

(Prep + Cook Time: 5 minutes / Servings: 4)

Nutritional Info per Serving:

Calories 150, Protein 10, Carbs 13, Fat 3

Ingredients:

2 cans of tuna, 5 oz. each

1 cup grated cheddar cheese

2 cups crushed saltine crackers

2 tbsp. butter

1 garlic clove, minced

Directions:

1. Set SAUTÉ mode. Melt the butter, and cook the garlic for 1 minute.
2. Add tuna, cheddar, and crackers.
3. Sauté for 2 minutes. Serve immediately and enjoy!

Stocks and Sauces

Fish Stock

(Prep + Cook Time: 65 minutes / Servings: 6)

Nutritional Info per Serving:

Calories 42, Protein 5.6, Carbs 0, Fat 2

Ingredients:

2 lemongrass stalks, chopped
1 cup chopped celery
1 cup chopped carrots
2 garlic cloves, minced

2 salmon heads, cut into quarters
1 tbsp. olive oil
Water
A handful of thyme

Directions:

1. Set the Instant Pot to SAUTÉ.
2. Heat the oil, and sauté the salmon heads for a couple of minutes.
3. Add the veggies and thyme. Pour water until it reaches 3 quarts.
4. Close the lid, select SOUP, and cook on HIGH for 45 minutes.
5. Release the pressure for 15 minutes. Strain the broth.

Beef Bone Broth

(Prep + Cook Time: 100 minutes / Servings: 4)

Nutritional Info per Serving:

Calories 18, Protein 2.9 Carbs 0, Fat 0.6

Ingredients:

2 bay leaves
2 thyme sprigs

3 oz. carrots, chopped
2 garlic cloves, minced

211

1 onion, chopped

1 ½ pounds beef bones

⅓ cup chopped celery

Salt and black pepper, to taste

Directions:

1. Place all of the ingredients into your Instant Pot.

2. Pour water just below the max line.

3. Close the lid, select MANUAL, and cook on HIGH for 90 minutes.

4. Allow pressure to release naturally.

5. Strain the broth.

Veggie Stock

(Prep + Cook Time: 45 minutes / Servings: 4)

Nutritional Info per Serving:

Calories 10, Protein 1, Carbs 0, Fat 1

Ingredients:

1 green onion, sliced

1 bay leaf

1 tsp. minced garlic

2 carrots, chopped

2 celery stalks, copped

3 parsley sprigs, chopped

2 thyme sprigs

3 black peppercorns

Salt and black pepper, to taste

water, as needed

Directions:

1. Place first 8 ingredients into your Instant Pot.

2. Pour water to just below the max line.

3. Close the lid, select SOUP, and cook for 30 minutes.

4. Allow pressure to release naturally.

5. Strain the broth and season with salt and pepper.

Chicken Stock

(Prep + Cook Time: 140 minutes / Servings: 4)

Nutritional Info per Serving:

Calories 50, Protein 10, Carbs 1.5, Fat 3

Ingredients:

½ onion, chopped
1 tbsp. apple cider vinegar
1 chicken carcass

1 bay leaf
8 peppercorns
Salt and black pepper, to taste

Directions:

1. Place first 6 ingredients into your Instant Pot.
2. Add enough water to cover the pot below the max line.
3. Close the lid, select SOUP, and cook for 120 minutes.
4. Allow pressure to release naturally. Strain the stock.

Bolognese Sauce

(Prep + Cook Time: 15 minutes / Servings: 4)

Nutritional Info per Serving:

Calories 363, Protein 37, Carbs 24, Fat 9

Ingredients:

¼ cup chopped parsley
3 garlic cloves, minced
3 basil leaves, chopped

1 pound ground beef
1 can pasta sauce

Directions:

1. Place all of the ingredients into your Instant Pot. Stir to combine.
2. Select MANUAL, and cook on HIGH for 8 minutes.

3. Release the pressure quickly.

Tomato and Basil Sauce

(Prep + Cook Time: 40 minutes / Servings: 4)

Nutritional Info per Serving:

Calories 40, Protein 1.7, Carbs 5, Fat 1.5

Ingredients:

½ cup chopped basil
1 tbsp. olive oil
2 ½ lb. roma tomatoes, diced
1 tsp. garlic powder

½ onion, diced
1 tbsp. Italian seasoning
3 garlic cloves, minced
Salt and black pepper, to taste

Directions:

1. Set your Instant Pot to SAUTÉ.
2. Heat the olive oil and sauté the onions and garlic for about 4 - 5 minutes.
3. Stir in the remaining ingredients.
4. Close the Instant Pot, select MANUAL, and cook on HIGH for 10 minutes.
5. Release the pressure quickly.
6. Select SAUTÉ, and sauté for 5 minutes.
7. Serve and enjoy!

Marinara Lentil Sauce

(Prep + Cook Time: 25 minutes / Servings: 4)

Nutritional Info per Serving:

Calories 170, Protein 5, Carbs 14, Fat 0

Ingredients:

⅓ cup red lentils

14 oz. can crushed tomatoes

½ tsp. salt

1 ½ tsp. minced garlic

1 cup water

1 sweet potato, diced

Directions:

1. Set your Instant Pot to SAUTÉ.
2. Add lentils, sweet potato, garlic, and salt.
3. Sauté for 2 minutes.
4. Add tomatoes and water and stir to combine.
5. Close the lid, select MANUAL, and cook on HIGH for 13 minutes.
6. Allow pressure to release naturally.
7. Blend with a hand blender.
8. Serve and enjoy!

Apple Sauce

(Prep + Cook Time: 30 minutes / Servings: 4)

Nutritional Info per Serving:

Calories 70, Protein 0.5, Carbs 19, Fat 1.5

Ingredients:

Juice from ½ lemon

12 apples, quartered

¼ tsp. sea salt

2 tbsp. ghee

1 tbsp. honey

1 tbsp. cinnamon

1 cup water

Directions:

1. Place all of the ingredients in your Instant Pot.
2. Close the lid, select MANUAL, and cook on HIGH for 3 minutes.
3. Release the pressure naturally.
4. Transfer all of the solids and half the cooking liquid to your blender.
5. Blend until smooth.

6. Serve and enjoy!

Pizza Dip

(Prep + Cook Time: 10 minutes / Servings: 8)

Nutritional Info per Serving:

Calories 187, Protein 7.5, Carbs 24.5, Fat 16.3

Ingredients:

1 ½ cups tomato sauce
1 ½ cups cream cheese
2 eggs, beaten

2 ½ cups mozzarella cheese
1 tsp. thyme, dried
2 tbsp. parsley, dried

Directions:

1. In a large bowl, mix the eggs, cream cheese, thyme, parsley, and pepper.
2. Pour the mixture into the stainless steel insert.
3. Add tomato sauce and mozzarella. Select MANUAL and cook on HIGH pressure for 5 minutes. Perform a quick release.

Cheese and Spinach Dip

(Prep + Cook Time: 10 minutes / Servings: 8)

Nutritional Info per Serving:

Calories 280, Protein 7.3, Carbs 23.8, Fat 25.3

Ingredients:

2 ½ cups cream cheese
1 ½ cups baby spinach, torn, rinsed
and drained

1 ½ cups mozzarella cheese
2 tsp. Italian seasoning
½ cup scallions

Directions:

1. Mix well all ingredients in a large bowl and transfer to the Instant Pot.
2. Press MANUAL and cook on HIGH pressure for 5 minutes.
3. Release the steam naturally.

Mexican Chili Dip

(Prep + Cook Time: 12 minutes / Servings: 5)

Nutritional Info per Serving:

Calories 216, Protein 5.3, Carbs 7.1, Fat 20.5

Ingredients:

1 cup tomato sauce
1 cup sour cream
1 cup cream cheese

1 tsp. dried oregano
1 tsp. ground cayenne pepper
1 tsp. ground chili pepper

Directions:

1. Combine all ingredients in a large bowl and stir well.
2. Pour the mixture into the Instant Pot.
3. Select MANUAL and cook on HIGH pressure for 8 minutes.

Broccoli Sauce

(Prep + Cook Time: 12 minutes / Servings: 7)

Nutritional Info per Serving:

Calories 253, Protein 10.3, Carbs 14.5, Fat 23.1

Ingredients:

1 ½ cups broccoli, chopped
1 ½ cups cheddar cheese, shredded
1 ½ cups cream cheese

1 tsp. garlic powder
2 tsp. parsley, dried
1 ½ cups chicken broth

Directions:

1. Mix all ingredients in a large bowl and stir well.
2. Transfer the mixture into the Instant Pot.
3. Select MANUAL and cook on HIGH pressure for 8 minutes.
4. When done, press CANCEL and allow for a natural release.

Creamy Basil Sauce

(Prep + Cook Time: 10 minutes / Servings: 4)

Nutritional Info per Serving:

Calories 263, Protein 9.7, Carbs 3.1, Fat 25.3

Ingredients:

1 cup cream cheese
3 tsp. parmesan cheese, shredded
1 cup fresh basil, torn

1 tbsp. olive oil
salt and black pepper

Directions:

1. Combine all ingredients in a large bowl. Stir well and transfer the mixture to the Pot.
2. Select MANUAL and cook on LOW pressure for 6 minutes.
3. Release the steam naturally.

Garlic Cheese Sauce

(Prep + Cook Time: 15 minutes / Servings: 6)

Nutritional Info per Serving:

Calories 330, Protein 12, Carbs 4.5, Fat 25

Ingredients:

1 ¼ cups cream cheese
1 ¼ cups cheddar cheese, shredded

1 ¼ cups chicken broth
2 tbsp. garlic powder

½ cup fresh parsley, chopped   ½ tsp. ground thyme, dried

Directions:

1. Combine all ingredients in a mixing bowl and stir well.
2. Transfer the mixture to the Instant Pot and press the WARM button and the cook for 9 minutes.

Cranberry Sauce

(Prep + Cook Time: 16 minutes / Servings:4)

Nutritional Info per Serving:

Calories 105, Protein 0.2, Carbs 27, Fat 0.1

Ingredients:

2 cups cranberries
1 tsp. orange zest, freshly grated
½ cup orange juice, freshly juiced

¼ cup brown sugar
2 tbsp. maple syrup

Directions:

1. Plug in your Instant Pot, and add cranberries in the stainless steel insert. Add maple syrup and orange juice, and stir well to combine. Sprinkle with orange zest, and close the lid. Adjust the steam release handle and, select MANUAL. Set timer for 1 minute, and cook on HIGH pressure.
2. When done, press Cancel button, and release the pressure naturally. Carefully open the lid.
3. Now, press Sauté button, and stir all well. Add brown sugar, and stir until thick sauce mixture is formed. Turn off the heat and transfer the sauce to the serving dish.
4. Serve cold.

Cheese Vegetables Sauce

(Prep + Cook Time: 15 minutes / Servings: 4)

Nutritional Info per Serving:

Calories 257, Protein 16.1, Carbs 41.5, Fat 8.1

Ingredients:

2 potatoes, peeled and chopped
2 carrots, sliced
3 cups water
1 onion, chopped
1 tbsp. turmeric, ground

1 tbsp. salt
1 garlic cloves, chopped
½ cup cashews, chopped
1 cup yeast

Directions:

1. Place all ingredients in the Pot. Close the lid and set the steam release handle.

2. Press MANUAL and cook on HIGH pressure and set timer for 6 minutes.

3. Perform a quick steam release

4. Let it cool and transfer to a blender, and blend until creamy.

5. Can be stored in airtight container, and refrigerated up to 8 days.

Tomato Barbecue Sauce

(Prep + Cook Time: 10 minutes / Servings: 4)

Nutritional Info per Serving:

Calories 137, Protein 3.1, Carbs 34.3, Fat 1.1

Ingredients:

1 ½ cups tomatoes, diced
3 tsp. brown sugar
1 cup ketchup
2 tsp. lemon juice, juiced

2 tbsp. onion powder
½ cup apple cider vinegar
1 tbsp. garlic powder
1 tbsp. dried oregano

1 tbsp. salt

Directions:

1. Place all ingredients in the stainless steel insert.
2. Close the lid and adjust the handle.
3. Press MANUAL and cook on HIGH for 6 minutes.
4. Allow for a natural release.

Green Hot Jalapeno Sauce

(Prep + Cook Time: 7 minutes / Servings: 6)

Nutritional Info per Serving:

Calories 32, Protein 1.1, Carbs 5.6, Fat 0.3

Ingredients:

7 oz. green jalapeno peppers, diced
3 garlic cloves, crushed
2 tsp. apple cider vinegar
2 green bell pepper, chopped

1 tbsp. sea salt
1 cup white vinegar
¼ cup water

Directions:

1. Place all ingredients in the Instant Pot.
2. Close the lid and adjust the handle.
3. Press MANUAL and cook on HIGH for 2 minutes.
4. Once done, click CANCEL and release the steam naturally.
5. Transfer to a blender and blend until well combined.
6. Store the sauce in small jars.

Beet and Squash Sauce

(Prep + Cook Time: 40 minutes / Servings: 4)

Nutritional Info per Serving::

Calories 139, Protein 3.7, Carbs 32.4, Fat 1.9

Ingredients:

4 small beets, cubed
4 carrots, cubed
2 ½ cups butternut squash, cubed
1 tbsp. dried basil

2 tsp. dried parsley
1 tbsp. dried oregano,
1 tsp. garlic powder
black pepper and salt

Directions:

1. Add all vegetables in the Instant Pot.
2. Pour in 2 ½ cups of water, and close the lid.
3. Press STEAM and cook on HIGH pressure for 12 minutes.
4. Allow for a natural pressure release.
5. Transfer to a food processor, and blend until creamy.
6. Add the spices and blend for another minute.
7. Transfer back to the Pot and click SAUTÉ for 15 minutes, stirring from time to time.

Salted Caramel Sauce

(Prep + Cook Time: 20 minutes / Servings: 4)

Nutritional Info per Serving:

Calories 40, Protein 0, Carbs 6, Fat 1.5

Ingredients:

½ tsp. vanilla
3 tbsp. butter
½ tsp. sea salt

1 cup sugar
⅓ cup heavy cream
⅓ cup water

Directions:

1. Combine the sugar and water in your Instant Pot.

2. Select SAUTÉ, and sauté for 13 minutes.

3. Stir in the remaining ingredients.

4. Whisk until the sauce becomes smooth.

5. Immediately remove to a heat-safe glass container, and let cool completely.

6. Serve and enjoy!

Vegan White Sauce

(Prep + Cook Time: 20 minutes / Servings: 4)

Nutritional Info per Serving:

Calories 39, Protein 3, Carbs 5, Fat 10

Ingredients:

½ cup water
12 oz. cauliflower florets

¼ tsp. garlic salt
2 tbsp. almond milk

Directions:

1. Combine the water, cauliflower, salt, and black pepper, in your Instant Pot.

2. Close the lid, select MANUAL, and cook for 3 minutes.

3. Allow pressure to release naturally. Blend with a hand blender.

4. Stir in the almond milk. Serve and enjoy!

Chili Sauce

(Prep + Cook Time: 25 minutes / Servings: 6)

Nutritional Info per Serving:

Calories 2, Protein 1, Carbs 0.7, Fat 0

Ingredients:

6 oz. hot peppers, stems removed
½ cup apple cider vinegar

Directions:

1. Set the Instant Pot to SAUTÉ mode.
2. Chop the peppers and place them in your Instant Pot.
3. Add a splash of vinegar and sauté for 3 minutes.
4. Close the lid, select MANUAL, and cook on HIGH for 1 minute.
5. Allow pressure to release naturally. Blend the sauce with a hand blender.

Desserts

Sweet Tapioca Pudding

(Prep + Cook Time: 10 minutes / Servings: 4)

Nutritional Info per Serving:

Calories 187, Protein 2.5, Carbs 39, Fat 2.5

Ingredients:

1 ¼ cups almond milk
⅓ cup sugar
⅓ cup tapioca pearls

⅓ cup sugar
½ cup water
½ tsp. vanilla extract

Directions:

1. Pour the water into your Instant Pot.
2. In a heatproof bowl, combine all of the remaining ingredients.
3. Place the bowl inside your Instant Pot.
4. Close the lid, select MANUAL, and cook on HIGH for 8 minutes.
5. Release the pressure naturally.
6. Serve and enjoy!

Date Toffee

(Prep + Cook Time: 45 minutes / Servings: 4)

Nutritional Info per Serving:

Calories 480, Protein 4, Carbs 60, Fat 20

Ingredients:

¾ cup chopped dates
¾ cup flour

1 egg
½ cup brown sugar

½ cup boiling water

2 tbsp. blackstrap molasses

½ tsp. vanilla extract

1 ½ cups water

Pinch of salt

½ tsp. baking powder

Directions:

1. Mix the sugar and butter until fluffy.
2. Combine the dry ingredients in one bowl.
3. In another bowl, combine the boiling water, dates, and molasses.
4. Gradually mix the date mixture and dry ingredients into the butter mixture.
5. Grease 4 ramekins.
6. Divide the mixture between them.
7. Pour the water into your Instant Pot, and place the ramekins on the rack.
8. Close the lid, select MANUAL, and cook on HIGH for 25 minutes.
9. Serve and enjoy!

Dark Chocolate Fondue

(Prep + Cook Time: 5 minutes / Servings: 4)

Nutritional Info per Serving:

Calories 216, Protein 2, Carbs 11, Fat 20

Ingredients:

2 cups water

1 tsp. sugar

3 ½ oz. coconut cream

8 oz. dark chocolate, chopped

Directions:

1. Pour the water into your Instant Pot.
2. In a heatproof bowl, add the chocolate, sugar, and coconut cream.
3. Place in the Instant Pot.
4. Close the lid, select MANUAL, and cook for 2 minutes.
5. Stir to combine.

Dark Chocolate Custard

(Prep + Cook Time: 55 minutes / Servings: 6)

Nutritional Info per Serving:

Calories 540, Protein 9, Carbs 50, Fat 36.5

Ingredients:

1 tsp. vanilla

13 oz. dark chocolate, chopped

6 egg yolks, whisked

½ cup sugar

4 cups water

1 cup milk

Directions:

1. Place all of the ingredients, except the water, into your Instant pot.
2. Cook on SAUTÉ until the sugar is dissolved.
3. Transfer the mixture to a baking dish.
4. Pour the water into the Instant Pot, and place the dish on the trivet.
5. Seal the lid, select MANUAL, and cook on HIGH for 30 minutes.
6. Release the pressure naturally. Serve and enjoy!

Simple Mango-Flavored Cake

(Prep + Cook Time: 50 minutes / Servings: 4)

Nutritional Info per Serving:

Calories 460, Protein 4, Carbs 78, Fat 14

Ingredients:

1 ¼ cups flour

¼ cup coconut oil

1 tsp. mango syrup

1 tsp. baking powder

Pinch of salt

¼ tsp. baking soda

¾ cup milk

2 cups water

½ cup sugar

Directions:

1. Grease a baking pan with cooking spray.
2. Pour the water in your Instant Pot.
3. Whisk together all of the remaining ingredients, in a bowl.
4. Transfer the batter to the prepared baking pan.
5. Place on the trivet. Close the lid, and select MANUAL.
6. Cook on HIGH for 35 minutes. Release the pressure quickly.

Bundt Cake with Bananas and Chocolate Chips

(Prep + Cook Time: 75 minutes / Servings: 6)

Nutritional Info per Serving:

Calories 232, Protein 3, Carbs 30, Fat 13

Ingredients:

1 cup buttermilk
1 ½ cups flour
2 bananas, mashed
¼ cup honey
1 tsp. baking soda

½ tsp. cinnamon
2 eggs
⅓ cup chocolate chips
⅔ cup water
Pinch of nutmeg

Directions:

1. Butter a Bundt pan. Pour the water into your Instant Pot.
2. Whisk together the wet ingredients along with the bananas, in one bowl.
3. Combine the dry ingredients, in another.
4. Combine the two mixtures gently. Pour the batter into the Bundt pan.
5. Place the cake in the Instant Pot.
6. Close the lid, select MANUAL, and cook on HIGH for 25 minutes.
7. Serve and enjoy!

French Squash Pie

(Prep + Cook Time: 35 minutes / Servings: 7)

Nutritional Info per Serving:

Calories 196, Protein 7.5, Carbs 54, Fat 14.6

Ingredients:

1 pack short cut pastry
14 oz. mashed squash
7 fl oz. whole milk
4 medium eggs

3/4 cup granulated sugar
1 tsp. cinnamon, ground
1 tsp. nutmeg
1 tsp. salt

Directions:

1. In a large bowl, add the pumpkin, milk, cinnamon, nutmeg, eggs, salt, and sugar. Whisk well.
2. Grease the bottom of the Instant Pot.
3. Carefully place she short cut pastry, forming edges with hands.
4. Pour the squash mixture inside the pastry and flatten the surface with a spatula.
5. Close the lid and release the handle.
6. Press MANUAL and cook for 25 minutes.
7. Perform a quick release.
8. Remove the pie from the pot, transfer to a serving platter and refrigerate overnight.

Cheese Cake

(Prep + Cook Time: 60 minutes / Servings: 6)

Nutritional Info per Serving:

Calories 325, Protein 15.1, Carbs 62.8, Fat 5.3

Ingredients:

3 eggs
1 ½ lb. yogurt
2 ½ cups sugar
2 tbsp. lemon zest

1 tbsp. lemon extract
½ tbsp. salt
1 cheesecake crust

For the Topping:

8 oz. cranberries, dried
3 tsp. cranberry jam
2 tbsp. lemon zest

1 tbsp. vanilla sugar
1 tbsp. cranberry extract
1 cup lukewarm water

Directions:

1. Preheat your oven to 340 degrees F.
2. In a large bowl, combine yogurt, sugar, eggs, lemon zest, lemon extract, salt. and beat with an electric mixer.
3. Grease a medium-sized spring form pan with oil. Place the crust and pour in the beaten filling. Flatten the surface if necessary, using a spatula.
4. Refrigerate for 30 minutes.
5. In the meantime, prepare the topping by combining the cranberries, cranberry jam, cranberry extract, vanilla sugar, lemon zest, and water, in a small pan.
6. Bring to a boil and let simmer for 20 minutes over low heat.
7. Fill your Instant Pot with water - about half inch, and position a rack at the bottom.
8. Place the cheesecake on the rack and add the cranberries' topping.
9. Cover the stainless steel insert with a double layer of paper towels and the lid.
10. Turn on your Instant Pot and set the steam release handle.
11. Press MANUAL and the time to 20 minutes.
12. Once done, turn off the heat and let cool in the Pot for about an hour.
13. Refrigerate the cheesecake overnight.

Apple Pie

(Prep + Cook Time: 40 minutes / Servings: 6)

Nutritional Info per Serving:

Calories 223, Protein 5.1, Carbs 29.3, Fat 11.6

Ingredients:

2 lb. apples, peeled and cut into pieces
1 egg, beaten, for brushing
⅓ cup granulated sugar
1 tbsp. vanilla sugar

⅓ cup breadcrumbs
Pie dough
3 tsp. cinnamon, ground
⅓ cup oil
⅓ cup all-purpose flour

Directions:

1. In a large bowl, mix apples, breadcrumbs, vanilla sugar, granulated sugar, and cinnamon; set aside.
2. Sprinkle flour on a surface and roll out the pie dough making 2 circle-shaped crusts.
3. Grease your Instant Pot with oil and place inside 1 piecrust.
4. Top with the apple mixture, and cover with the other circle-shaped crust.
5. Crimp the edges to complete the seal, and brush it with the egg.
6. Sprinkle the pie with powdered sugar.
7. Close the lid, and set the steam release handle.
8. Press MANUAL and cook for 20 minutes. Release the steam naturally.
9. Let it covered for a while. Then serve and enjoy.

Fig Spread Dessert

(Prep + Cook Time: 35 minutes / Servings: 12)

Nutritional Info per Serving:

Calories 265, Protein 2,5, Carbs 31.6, Fat 15.1

Ingredients:

1 cup all-purpose flour
3/4 cup vegetable oil
3/4 cup milk
3/4 cup lukewarm water

⅓ cup corn flour
⅓ cup fig spread
⅓ cup wheat groats
2 tsp. of baking powder

For the Topping:

1 ½ cups brown sugar
⅓ cup of fig spread

2 cups of water

Directions:

1. Prepare the topping first, so it is cool before using it.
2. In a heavy-bottomed pot, add sugar, fig spread, and water. Bring to a boil over high heat. Cook for 4 minutes, stirring constantly.
3. Remove from the heat and let cool.
4. In another pot, add oil, lukewarm water, milk, and the fig spread. Bring to a boil, and then add flour, wheat groats, corn flour, and baking powder. Mix well and stir.
5. Cook for 4 to 5 more minutes. Cool well and form the dough.
6. With your hands, shape 2-inch thick balls, about 12 of them.
7. Carefully flatten the surface and transfer to a greased Instant Pot.
8. Set the steam release handle. Press MANUAL and set to 10 minutes.
9. Perform a quick release.
10. Remove the fig spread and top with the cold topping.
11. Refrigerate before servings.

Crème Brûlée

(Prep + Cook Time: 12 minutes / Servings: 4)

Nutritional Info per Serving:

Calories 231, Protein 14.5, Carbs 19.1, Fat 10.3

Ingredients:

8 egg yolks

5 cups of heavy cream

1 vanilla bean, split lengthwise

1 ¼ cups sugar, divided

Directions:

1. In a large bowl, combine the egg yolks, heavy cream and 1 cup of sugar. Beat with electric mixer.

2. Scrape the seeds out of the vanilla bean and add them to the heavy cream mixture. Add salt and beat again.

3. Pour the mixture into four standard-sized ramekins; set aside.

4. Take 4x12 inches long pieces of aluminum foil, and roll them up in snake-shaped pieces.

5. Curl into a circles, pinching the ends together.

6. Place at the bottom of the Instant Pot.

7. Place each ramekin on aluminum circle, and pour water to cover ⅓ of the way. Press MANUAL and cook o HIGH pressure for 7 minutes.

8. Allow for a natural pressure release for 10 minutes, and then perform a quick release.

9. Remove the ramekins from the Pot, and add 1 tbsp. of sugar in each ramekin. Burn the surface with a culinary torch until lightly brown. Serve cool.

Sweet Pumpkin Pudding

(Prep + Cook Time: 30 minutes / Servings: 6)

Nutritional Info per Serving:

Calories 295, Protein 1.8, Carbs 68.1, Fat 0.8

Ingredients:

1 lb. pumpkin, peeled, seeded, chopped into pieces

6 cups pumpkin juice

1 ½ cups cornstarch

1 ½ cups granulated sugar

4 cloves

1 tbsp. cinnamon, ground

Directions:

1. Place the pumpkin in the Instant Pot.
2. In a bowl, combine the sugar with pumpkin juice.
3. Beat well until the sugar dissolves completely.
4. Add the mixture to the Pot and add in 1 cup of cornstarch, cinnamon, cloves, and stir. Close the lid, and select MANUAL and the timer to 10 minutes.
5. Perform a quick release. Open and pour the pudding into 6 serving bowls.
6. Let cool and refrigerate overnight.

Vanilla Pie-Cake

(Prep + Cook Time: 20 minutes / Servings: 6)

Nutritional Info per Serving:

Calories 516, Protein 12.1, Carbs 75.1, Fat 16.9

Ingredients:

3 pie crusts
16 oz. bag chocolate chips
3 ½ cups milk

⅓ cup walnuts, minced
⅓ cup granulated sugar
½ cup vanilla pudding powder

Directions:

1. Press the SAUTÉ button, and add the vanilla pudding powder, sugar and milk.
2. Cook until it thickens, stirring constantly; then remove from the Instant Pot.
3. Place one crust at the bottom of a spring form pan.
4. Pour half of the pudding, and sprinkle with chocolate chips and minced walnuts. Cover with another crust, and repeat the process.
5. Then wrap in foil. Place the spring form pan in the Pot, and seal the lid.
6. Press MANUAL and set to 3 minutes. Perform a quick release.

7. Remove the cake and refrigerate overnight.

Wild Berries Pancakes

(Prep + Cook Time: 20 minutes / Servings: 4)

Nutritional Info per Serving:

Calories 151, Protein 8.8 g, Carbs 21.1 g, Fat 2.6 g

Ingredients:

1 cup buckwheat flour
2 tbsp. baking powder
1 ½ cups skim milk
1 egg

1 tsp. salt
1 tbsp. vanilla sugar
1 cup yogurt
1 cup fresh wild berries

Directions:

1. In a medium-sized bowl, mix the milk and the egg, and beat with an electric mixer until foamy. Gradually add flour, and continue to beat.
2. Add baking powder, vanilla sugar and salt.
3. Keep beating 3 more minutes until batter is formed.
4. Grease the stainless steel insert with oil. Spoon 3 tbsp. of batter into the pot for every pancake.
5. Close the lid, and press MANUAL. Cook on LOW pressure for 5 minutes.
6. Perform a quick release. Repeat the process with the remaining batter.
7. Top each pancake with 1 tbsp. of yogurt and wild berries. Serve warm.

Blueberry Strudel

(Prep + Cook Time: 45 minutes / Servings: 6)

Nutritional Info per Serving:

Calories 163, Protein 7.1, Carbs 15.7, Fat 8.1

Ingredients:

1 cup fresh raspberries
1 cup fresh blueberries
1 cup soft cream cheese
2 eggs, beaten

2 puff pastry sheets
2 tbsp. powdered stevia
2 tbsp. butter, softened
⅓ cup cornstarch

Directions:

1. In a food processor, place the blueberries, stevia, cornstarch, and salt.
2. Blend until smooth, and transfer to a heavy-bottomed pot. Add 1 cup of water, and bring it to a boil.
3. Cook for 3 minutes, stirring constantly.
4. Remove from the heat and let cool.
5. Unfold the pastry, and cut each sheet into 4x7-inches pieces.
6. Brush with the half of the beaten eggs. Place 2 tbsp. of cream cheese along with 2 tbsp. of blueberry mixture in the middle of each pastry.
7. Fold the sheets and brush with the remaining eggs.
8. Cut the surface and carefully place each strudel into the Instant Pot.
9. Press MANUAL and cook on LOW pressure for 25 minutes.
10. Allow for a natural pressure release. Cool for 10 minutes.
11. Transfer the strudels to a serving plate with the help of a spatula.

Vanilla Pancakes

(Prep + Cook Time: 35 minutes / Servings: 6)

Nutritional Info per Serving:

Calories 193, Protein 7.1, Carbs 26.8, Fat 5.8

Ingredients:

2 bananas, mashed
2 eggs
1 ½ cups rolled oats

1 cup goat milk
2 tbsp. coconut oil
1 tbsp. baking powder

1 tbsp. vanilla extract   pinch of salt
1 tbsp. honey   cooking spray

Directions:

1. Place all ingredients in a blender, and blend until completely smooth batter.
2. Grease the stainless steel insert with cooking spray.
3. Add ¼ cup of the batter and close the lid.
4. Press MANUAL and cook on low pressure for 5 minutes.
5. Repeat the process with the remaining batter.
6. Serve immediately with honey or jam.

Peach Crumb

(Prep + Cook Time: 55 minutes / Servings: 6)

Nutritional Info per Serving:

Calories 510, Protein 2.5, Carbs 70, Fat 27

Ingredients:

1 tsp. cinnamon   ½ cup sugar
⅔ cup breadcrumbs   Juice and zest of ½ lemon
¾ cup melted butter   1 tsp. grated ginger
6 small peaches, sliced   1 ½ cups water

Directions:

1. Pour the water into your Instant Pot.
2. Combine the butter, crumbs, cinnamon, lemon juice, zest, ginger, and sugar in a bowl. Grease a baking pan.
3. Arrange a layer of the peaches at the bottom of the pan.
4. Top with the part of the crumb mixture.
5. Repeat the process until you have used all ingredients.
6. Place the pan in the Instant Pot.

7. Close the lid, select MANUAL, and cook on HIGH for 23 minutes.

8. Release the pressure naturally. Serve and enjoy!

Instant Apple Dumplings

(Prep + Cook Time: 35 minutes / Servings: 6)

Nutritional Info per Serving:

Calories 267, Protein 4, Carbs 40, Fat 5

Ingredients:

1 tsp. cinnamon

4 tbsp. butter

8 oz. crescent rolls

¾ cup apple cider

1 apple, cut into 8 wedges

½ tsp. vanilla

½ cup brown sugar

Directions:

1. Cut the crescent roll into 8 pieces, and roll each of the pieces around the apple wedges to form dumplings. Melt butter in your Instant Pot on SAUTÉ.

2. Add vanilla, sugar, and cinnamon, and cook for 1 minute.

3. Add the dumplings, and pour the cider over.

4. Close the lid, select MANUAL, and cook on HIGH for 10 minutes.

5. Release the pressure naturally.

Ricotta Cake with Apples

(Prep + Cook Time: 5 minutes / Servings: 4)

Nutritional Info per Serving:

Calories 463, Protein 13, Carbs 60, Fat 20

Ingredients:

¼ cup sugar

2 apples, one diced and one sliced

1 egg

1 cup flour

1 cup ricotta

3 tbsp. oil

2 tsp. baking powder

1 tbsp. lemon juice

1 tsp. baking soda

1 tsp. vanilla

Directions:

1. Pour 2 cups of water into your Instant Pot.
2. Line a baking dish with parchment paper.
3. Arrange the sliced apples at the bottom. Sprinkle with lemon juice.
4. Whisk the remaining ingredients in a bowl, including the diced apple.
5. Pour the batter over the apples.
6. Place the pan in the Instant Pot.
7. Close the lid, select MANUAL, and cook on HIGH for 20 minutes.
8. Do a quick pressure release.
9. Serve and enjoy!

Blackberry Jam

(Prep + Cook Time: 30 minutes / Servings: 2 Pints)

Nutritional Info per Serving (1 tbsp.):

Calories 180, Protein 1, Carbs 40, Fat 0

Ingredients:

2 pounds blackberries

40 oz. honey

Directions:

1. Combine the ingredients in your Instant Pot.
2. Set the Instant Pot to KEEP WARM.
3. Let it sit for a couple of minutes, until the honey becomes liquid.
4. Then, turn on the SAUTÉ mode, and bring the mixture to a boil.
5. Close the lid, set MANUAL cooking mode, and cook for 2 minutes on HIGH.

6. Release the pressure naturally.
7. Set the Instant Pot to SAUTÉ again, and once again bring it to a boil.
8. Serve and enjoy!

Instant Brownies

(Prep + Cook Time: 45 minutes / Servings: 4)

Nutritional Info per Serving:

Calories 530, Protein 8, Carbs 75, Fat 25

Ingredients:

1 tbsp. honey
½ cup melted butter
1 cup sugar
¼ tsp. salt

¼ cup cocoa powder
¾ cup flour
2 eggs
¾ tsp. baking powder

Directions:

1. Pour 2 cups of water into your Instant Pot.
2. Mix the ingredients in a bowl, until well combined.
3. Grease a pan with cooking spray.
4. Pour the batter in it. Place it in your Instant Pot, and close the lid.
5. Choose MANUAL, and cook on HIGH for 35 minutes.
6. Do a quick pressure release.

Pressureless Simple Sponge Cake

(Prep + Cook Time: 70 minutes / Servings: 6)

Nutritional Info per Serving:

Calories 405, Protein 6, Carbs 45, Fat 20

Ingredients:

1 ¼ cups flour
½ cup canola oil
¾ tsp. vanilla powder
½ cup milk

1½ cups powdered sugar
2 eggs
1 ½ tsp. baking powder

Directions:

1. Grease a pan with cooking spray. Mix all of the ingredients in a bowl.
2. Transfer to the pan. Set your Instant Pot to SAUTÉ.
3. Place the cake in the Instant Pot, and bake for about 40 minutes.

Chocolate Molten Lava Cake

(Prep + Cook Time: 25 minutes / Servings: 4)

Nutritional Info per Serving:

Calories 528, Protein 6.6, Carbs 48 Fat 30

Ingredients:

½ cup powdered sugar
2 tsp. vanilla extract
8 tbsp. butter

4 tbsp. flour
2 eggs
1 cup chocolate chips, melted

Directions:

1. Pour 2 cups of water into your Instant Pot. Grease 4 ramekins.
2. Whisk all of the ingredients together in a bowl.
3. Transfer to the ramekins.
4. Arrange the ramekins on the trivet.
5. Close the lid, select MANUAL, and cook on HIGH for 7 minutes.
6. Release the pressure naturally.
7. Serve and enjoy!

Vanilla Egg Custard

(Prep + Cook Time: 25 minutes / Servings: 6)

Nutritional Info per Serving:

Calories 148, Protein 7, Carbs 16, Fat 6

Ingredients:

6 eggs

1 tsp. vanilla extract

¼ tsp. cinnamon

4 cups milk

1 ½ cups water

¾ cup sugar

Directions:

1. Pour the water into your Instant Pot. Beat the eggs in a bowl.
2. Whisk in the remaining ingredients.
3. Pour this mixture into 6 large, and previously greased ramekins.
4. Place them on the trivet.
5. Close the lid, select MANUAL, and cook for 7 minutes on HIGH.
6. Release the pressure naturally.

Instant Cinnamon Rice Pudding

(Prep + Cook Time: 30 minutes / Servings: 6)

Nutritional Info per Serving:

Calories 240, Protein 5, Carbs 38, Fat 7

Ingredients:

1 cup basmati rice

¾ cup heavy cream

Pinch of sea salt

¼ cup maple syrup

½ tsp. vanilla extract

1 tsp. cinnamon

2 cups milk

1 tsp. cinnamon

Directions:

1. Rinse the rice well, and add it to the Instant Pot.
2. Add the remaining ingredients, except the heavy cream.
3. Stir well. Close the lid, select PORRIDGE, and cook for 20 minutes.
4. Release the pressure naturally. Stir in the cream.
5. Serve and enjoy!

Rib-Eye Steak with Mustard

(Prep + Cook Time: 35 minutes / Servings: 4)

Nutritional Info per Serving:

Calories 553, Protein 32.8, Carbs 2.5, Fat 47.3

Ingredients:

4 rib-eye steak, boneless. at least
1-inch thick
3 cups beef broth

3 tbsp. Dijon mustard
3 tbsp. canola oil
juice of half lemon

Directions:

1. In a small bowl, mix the lemon juice, oil, Dijon mustard, salt and pepper.
2. Brush the steaks with the mixture; set aside.
3. Pour the beef broth into the Instant Pot.
4. Place steamer insert and arrange the steaks.
5. Seal, select STEAM button and set to 25 minutes.
6. When done, perform a quick release.
7. Remove the broth and press SAUTÉ. Brown the steaks on both sides for 4 to 5 minutes.

Chicken Drumstick Salad

(Prep + Cook Time: 75 minutes / Servings: 4)

Nutritional Info per Serving:

Calories 275, Protein 16.3, Carbs 10.1 Fat 18.3

Ingredients:

4 chicken drumsticks, around a pound

6 oz. button mushrooms, whole

3 cups chicken broth

3 oz. lettuce

1 tomato, diced

1 cucumber, sliced

3 tbsp. olive oil

1 tsp. Dijon mustard

¼ cup white wine

1 tbsp. squeezed lemon juice

1 tbsp. Italian seasoning mix

Directions:

1. In a bowl, mix the mustard, 2 tbsp. of olive oil, Italian seasoning mix, white wine and a pinch of salt.

2. Stir very well and brush the meat.

3. Wrap it up in aluminum foil and refrigerate for 35 minutes.

4. Meanwhile, grease the bottom of your Instant Pot with oil. Add the mushrooms and press SAUTÉ. Cook for 10 - 12 minutes, stirring occasionally.

5. To prepare the salad, place all vegetables in a serving bowl, including the mushrooms, and stir very well.

6. Remove the meat from the fridge and transfer into the pot.

7. Add in the chicken broth and seal the lid.

8. Set the steam release handle, select MEAT and cook for 15 minutes.

9. Once done, remove the drumsticks from the Pot and add them to a preheated non-stick pan. Brown for at least 5 minutes. Serve with the salad.

T-Bone Steak with Basil

(Prep + Cook Time: 65 minutes / Servings: 4)

Nutritional Info per Serving:

Calories 632, Protein 54.8, Carbs 2.5, Fat 42.5

Ingredients:

2. T-bone steaks, 1 lb. in total

2 tbsp. Dijon mustard

½ tsp. dried basil, crushed

¼ cup oil

1 tsp. Himalayan salt

½ tsp. ground black pepper

Directions:

1. Mix together the oil, mustard, basil, salt and black pepper.
2. Brush the steaks with the mixture and refrigerate for 45 minutes.
3. Set the steamer insert and pour in 3 cups of water.
4. Line the steaks in the steamer, close the lid and press STEAM.
5. Cook for 17 - 20 minutes.
6. Perform a quick release and remove the liquid from the stainless steel insert.
7. Press SAUTÉ and brown the steaks, one at a time for 6 minutes, turning once.

Crispy Trout with Mint

(Prep + Cook Time: 40 minutes / Servings: 2)

Nutritional Info per Serving:

Calories 552, Protein 45.6, Carbs 2.8, Fat 25.3

Ingredients:

2 pieces trout, 1 lb. in total
3 cups fish stock
3 garlic cloves, chopped
3 tbsp. extra-virgin olive oil
1 tsp. dried thyme, ground
1 tsp. fresh parsley, chopped

1 tsp. fresh mint, chopped
1 tsp. fresh lemon juice
1 tsp. fresh lime juice
1 tsp. red peppers flakes
1 tsp. sea salt

Directions:

1. Combine mint, parsley, thyme, chili, garlic, lemon juice, olive oil, lime juice and salt. Mix well.
2. Brush the fish with the marinade, both inside and outside; set aside.
3. Set the steamer insert and pour in the fish stock.
4. Place the fish in the insert. Close the lid and set the steam release handle.
5. Press STEAM and cook for 25 minutes.

6. Perform a quick release and carefully remove the fish.

Beef Steak with Salad

(Prep + Cook Time: 50 minutes / Servings: 4)

Nutritional Info per Serving:

Calories 363, Protein 28.1, Carbs 5.1, Fat 26.3

Ingredients:

1 lb. rib-eye steak, boneless
6 oz. fresh arugula
1 tomato, sliced
¼ cup fresh goat cheese
2 cups beef broth

2 tsp. red wine vinegar
1 tsp. Italian seasoning
3 tbsp. olive oil
1 oz. hazelnuts, crushed

Directions:

1. Mix together vinegar, Italian seasoning and 1 tbsp. olive oil.
2. Brush the meat and place in it the Instant Pot.
3. Set aside the remaining mixture.
4. Pour in beef broth and close the lid.
5. Set the steam release handle, press MEAT and cook for 17 - 20 minutes.
6. In the meantime, add together arugula, tomato, goat cheese and hazelnuts, in a large bowl. Mix well and set aside the salad.
7. Release the pressure naturally and remove the steaks and the broth.
8. Grease the stainless steel insert with oil and select SAUTÉ.
9. Brown the steaks on both sides for 4 - 5 minutes.
10. Let them cool for about 5 minutes before slicing.
11. Drizzle with red wine mixture and serve with the salad.

Steamed Tench

(Prep + Cook Time: 30 minutes / Servings: 6)

Nutritional Info per Serving:

Calories 252, Protein 21.4, Carbs 3.5, Fat 15.9

Ingredients:

1 tench, cleaned and gutted
1 lemon, sliced
3 tbsp. extra virgin olive oil
1 tbsp. fresh rosemary, chopped

¼ tbsp. thyme, dried
2 garlic cloves, crushed
pinch of sea salt

Directions:

1. In a bowl, mix olive oil, thyme, rosemary, garlic and salt. Stir well.
2. Brush the fish with the mixture and stuff with lemon slices.
3. Pour 4 cups of water into the stainless steel insert of the Instant Pot.
4. Set the steamer insert and place the fish in.
5. Cut in half if the fish is too big and won't fit.
6. Close the lid, set the handle and select SAUTÉ mode.
7. Cook for 15 minutes and perform a quick release.

Chicken with Mustard

(Prep + Cook Time: 40 minutes / Servings: 2)

Nutritional Info per Serving:

Calories 389, Protein 45, Carbs 5.8, Fat 17.5

Ingredients:

1 lb. chicken breasts, boneless and skinless
3 cups chicken stock

2 tbsp. olive oil
2 tbsp. Dijon mustard
¼ cup apple cider vinegar

Directions:

1. Place the chicken in your Instant Pot and pour in the chicken stock.

2. Press MEAT and cook for 20 minutes.
3. Perform a quick release and remove the ingredients.
4. In a small bowl, mix olive oil, mustard and apple cider.
5. Pour the mixture into the Pot and press SAUTÉ.
6. Arrange the meat in this mixture and cook for 12 minutes, turning once.
7. Serve the chicken with the sauce.

Quick Salmon Fillets

(Prep + Cook Time: 15 minutes / Servings: 4)

Nutritional Info per Serving:

Calories 413, Protein 42.1, Carbs 2.5 Fat 23.5

Ingredients:

4 salmon fillets
2 tbsp. butter, softened
2 tbsp. dill

juice from 2 lemons
salt and black pepper

Directions:

1. Season the fillets with salt and pepper.
2. Set the steamer insert of your Instant Pot and place the salmon in.
3. Pour in 3 cups of water and the lemon juice. Close the lid and set the steam release handle.
4. Cook on STEAM mode for 5 minutes.
5. Release the pressure naturally and remove the ingredients; set aside.
6. Press SAUTÉ mode and add butter.
7. Brown the fillets on both sides, for 5 minutes.
8. Remove from them the pot and sprinkle with dill.

Eggplant Casserole

(Prep + Cook Time: 30 minutes / Servings: 2)

Nutritional Info per Serving:

Calories 277, Protein 16.5, Carbs 56.7 Fat 8.5

Ingredients:

2 eggplants, peeled, cut lengthwise into thin sheets.
2 tomatoes, diced
1 cup ground beef

1 onion, chopped
1 tbsp. olive oil
salt and black pepper
¼ cup parsley, chopped

Directions:

1. Season the eggplants with salt. Leave them for 10 minutes, then rinse and drain.
2. Grease the stainless steel insert with oil.
3. Add onion and stir-fry for 3 minutes.
4. Add the ground beef and tomato, and cook for 6 more minutes.
5. Transfer into a deep bowl.
6. Lay eggplant slices (not all) on the bottom of the Pot.
7. Spread the ground beef mixture over and sprinkle with parsley. Make a second layer with eggplant slices, and repeat the process until you have all the ingredients inside.
8. Close the lid and set the steam release handle.
9. Select MANUAL and cook for 15 minutes.

Eggplants and Beef Stew

(Prep + Cook Time: 45 minutes / Servings: 6)

Nutritional Info per Serving (without the cheese)

Calories 185, Protein 17.5, Carbs 10.4, Fat 10.7

Ingredients:

8 oz. beef neck, chopped into pieces

1 eggplant, sliced

2 cups fire-roasted tomatoes

½ cup fresh green peas

1 cup beef broth

3 tbsp. olive oil

2 tsp. tomato paste

1 tbsp. cayenne pepper

½ tsp. of salt

shredded cheese

Directions:

1. Rub the beef chops with salt and cayenne pepper; set aside.
2. Grease the Instant Pot with olive oil and add the meat. Press SAUTÉ and cook for 7 - 8 minutes or until golden brown.
3. Add the remaining ingredients and seal the lid.
4. Adjust the steam release handle and select MEAT.
5. Cook for 35 minutes on HIGH pressure. Perform a quick release.
6. Make sure the pot stays covered for another 10 minutes before removing the lid.
7. Sprinkle with cheese, parmesan or cheddar before serving.
8. Serve and enjoy!

Chicken and Bell Peppers

(Prep + Cook Time: 20 minutes / Servings: 4)

Nutritional Info per Serving:

Calories 317, Protein 15.5, Carbs 31.5, Fat 11.6

Ingredients:

1 lb. chicken breasts, skinless and boneless, cut into pieces

2 large potatoes, peeled and chopped

4 bell peppers, chopped and seeded

2 carrots, sliced

3 cups chicken broth

1 tomato, diced

3 tbsp. extra virgin olive oil

1 tsp. cayenne pepper

¼ cup fresh parsley, chopped

2. Stir and cook for 2 minutes.
3. Add in potatoes, tomatoes and parsley. Stir well and add the chicke
4. Pour in the broth and close the lid.
5. Cook for 15 minutes on MEAT function.
6. Allow a natural pressure release.

Classic Ragout

(Prep + Cook Time: 25 minutes / Servings: 5)

Nutritional Info per Serving:

Calories 312, Protein 25.5, Carbs 21.5, Fat 13.7

Ingredients:

1 lb. lamb chops, cut into 1-inch thick pieces
1 cup peas, rinsed
3 carrots, chopped
2 onions, chopped

1 potato, peeled and chopped
1 tomato, peeled and diced
4 tbsp. of extra virgin olive oil,
1 tbsp. of cayenne pepper
salt and black pepper

Directions:

1. Grease the stainless steel insert with 1 tbsp. of oil and lay the mea
   bottom.
2. Add peas, onions, carrots, potatoes and tomato.
3. Sprinkle with 3 tbsp. of olive oil, cayenne pepper, salt and pepper.
4. Stir well and seal the lid.
5. Cook for 20 minutes on MEAT setting.
6. Press CANCEL and release the steam handle.
7. Let cool for 5 minutes before serving.

Spicy White Peas

(Prep + Cook Time: 30 minutes / Servings: 4)

Nutritional Info per Serving:

Calories 215, Protein 11, Carbs 26, Fat 10.4

Ingredients:

1 lb. of white peas
5 slices of bacon
2 bay leaves, dried
1 onion, chopped

1 chili pepper, chopped
1 tbsp. flour
2 tbsp. of butter
1 tsp. of cayenne pepper

Directions:

1. Melt butter in your Instant Pot on SAUTÉ mode button.

2. Add onion and stir-fry for 2 - 3 minutes or until translucent.

3. Add bacon, peas, bay leaves, chili pepper, salt and black pepper.

4. Stir in flour and add 3 cups of water.

5. Select MANUAL and set the timer to 15 minutes.

6. Release the steam naturally. Cool before serving.

Meatballs in Yogurt Dip

(Prep + Cook Time: 35 minutes / Servings: 4)

Nutritional Info per Serving:

Calories 466, Protein 42.3, Carbs 21.3, Fat 25.8

Ingredients:

1 lb. ground beef
2 garlic cloves, crushed
3 tbsp. extra virgin olive oil
1 tbsp. rosemary, crushed

1 egg, beaten
¼ cup flour
½ tsp. salt

For the dip:

2 cups liquid yogurt
2 tbsp. fresh parsley

1 cup Greek yogurt
1 garlic clove, crushed

Directions:

1. Greased the stainless steel insert.
2. In a bowl, combine the ground beef with garlic, rosemary, egg and salt. Mix very well. Shape 2-inches balls and transfer the Pot.
3. Add half cup of water. Press MEAT and cook for 15 minutes.
4. Meanwhile, combine the yogurts, parsley and crushed garlic.
5. Perform a quick release.
6. Remove from the pot, and serve cool with the yogurt dip drizzled over.

Spinach Pie

(Prep + Cook Time: 25 minutes / Servings: 4)

Nutritional Info per Serving:

Calories 303, Protein 15.1, Carbs 12.8, Fat 25.1

Ingredients:

1 pack pie dough, 6 sheets
1 lb. spinach, rinsed and chopped
3 eggs, beaten
2 tbsp. of butter
½ cup mascarpone cheese

½ cup feta cheese, shredded
½ cup goat cheese
½ cup milk
Oil for greasing the pot

Directions:

1. In a large bowl, combine the eggs, spinach, mascarpone, feta and goat cheese; set aside.

2. Dust flour on a clean surface and unfold the of pie dough sheet. Using a rolling pin, roll the dough to fit the Instant Pot. Repeat the process with all 6 sheets.

3. In a skillet, combine milk and butter. Bring to a boil and let the butter to melt completely; remove from heat.

4. Grease the bottom of your Instant Pot with oil.

5. Line parchment paper and place two pie sheets.

6. Brush with the milk mixture. Add in a layer of the spinach mixture and cover with another 2 pie sheets. Brush with butter again and more milk mixture, repeating the process until all the ingredients are used.

7. Close the lid and set the steam release handle.

8. Press MANUAL and cook for 7 minutes. Perform a quick release.

9. Let it cool for 10 minutes before transferring to a plate.

Greek Lasagna

(Prep + Cook Time: 30 minutes / Servings: 4)

Nutritional Info per Serving:

Calories 256, Protein 12.5, Carbs 16.5, Fat 13.6

Ingredients:

1 eggplant, sliced
4 oz. mozzarella, sliced
3 oz. cream cheese
2 tomatoes, sliced

¼ cup olive oil
salt and black pepper
1 tsp. oregano, dried

Directions:

1. Grease the Pot with olive oil. Lay eggplant slices on the bottom.

2. Add one slice of mozzarella, then a tomato slice. Top with cream cheese.

3. Repeat until all the ingredients are used.

4. Mix olive oil, salt, pepper and oregano. Pour over the lasagna and add half cup of water. Close the lid and set the release steam.
5. Press MANUAL and cook for 5 minutes.
6. Perform a natural release and enjoy.

Lamb Stew with Vegetables

(Prep + Cook Time: 50 minutes / Servings: 4)

Nutritional Info per Serving:

Calories 382, Protein 33.6, Carbs 27.1, Fat 16.1

Ingredients:

1 lb. lamb neck, boneless
2 potatoes, peeled and chopped into pieces
2 carrots, sliced
1 tomato, diced

1 red bell pepper, chopped
3 garlic cloves
2 tbsp. extra virgin olive oil
juice from 1 lemon
fresh parsley, chopped

Directions:

1. Grease the Instant Pot with olive oil.
2. Place the meat at the bottom, add the other ingredients and 2 cups of water.
3. Add a handful of fresh parsley and seal the lid.
4. Set the steam release handle and select MANUAL for 40 minutes.
5. Perform a quick release.

Whole Chicken with Veggies

(Prep + Cook Time: 45 minutes / Servings: 4)

Nutritional Info per Serving:

Calories 295, Protein 33, Carbs 36, Fat 11

Ingredients:

1 whole chicken, 3 lb.
8 oz. of fresh broccoli
6 oz. cauliflower florets
1 onion, chopped
1 potato, peeled and chopped
3 carrots, sliced

1 tomato, peeled and diced
handful of yellow wax beans, whole
hfandful of fresh parsley, chopped
¼ cup olive oil, divided
salt and black pepper
1 tsp. cayenne pepper

Directions:

1. Grease the Instant Pot with 3 tbsp. olive oil. Press SAUTÉ and add onion.

2. Stir-fry it for 4 to 5 minutes. Add the carrots and cook for 5 more minutes.

3. Add the remaining oil, vegetables, salt, black pepper, cayenne pepper, and place the chicken on top.

4. Pour in a cup of water and close the lid.

5. Select MANUAL and cook on HIGH pressure for 30 minutes.

6. Allow for a natural pressure release.

Beef Stroganoff

(Prep + Cook Time: 40 minutes / Servings: 5)

Nutritional Info per Serving:

Calories 323, Protein 23.1, Carbs 12.7, Fat 22.5

Ingredients:

1 lb. beef steak, cut into pieces
1 cup mushrooms, sliced
1 cup sour cream
2 cups beef broth
2 tbsp. Worcestershire sauce

3 tbsp. olive oil
2 garlic cloves, minced
1 tbsp. flour
1 onion, sliced
salt and black pepper

Directions:

1. In a bowl, mix flour with salt and black pepper.

2. Coat the meat and place it in your greased Instant Pot.

3. Close the lid and cook on LOW pressure for 11 minutes.

4. Add mushrooms, onion, garlic, beef broth and drizzle with Worcestershire sauce. Seal the lid and select MANUAL.

5. Set the steam release handle and the timer to 19 minutes on HIGH pressure.

6. Perform a quick release.

7. Press CANCEL and open the lid and add in the sour cream. Let covered for 10 minutes.

Meatloaf with Herbs

(Prep + Cook Time: 45 minutes / Servings: 6)

Nutritional Info per Serving:

Calories 436, Protein 43.1, Carbs 35.4, Fat 23.8

Ingredients:

2 lb. ground beef

1 cup flour

2 eggs

2 tbsp. olive oil

½ tsp. minced garlic

1 tsp. thyme, dried

1 tsp. dried rosemary, ground

salt

Directions:

1. In a bowl, combine the meat, flour, eggs, thyme, rosemary and salt.

2. Mix with hands and set aside.

3. Grease the Instant Pot with olive oil.

4. Form meatloaf on the bottom of the pot.

5. Close the lid and set the steam release.

6. Select MEAT and cook on HIGH for 40 minutes.

7. Perform a quick release.

8. Serve with salad or potatoes.

Quinoa Stew

(Prep + Cook Time: 25 minutes / Servings: 4)

Nutritional Info per Serving:

Calories 273, Protein 16.5, Carbs 45.3, Fat 12.1

Ingredients:

1 cup quinoa, soaked overnight

1 cup white lentils, soaked overnight

1 cup tomatoes, diced

3 cups beef broth

¼ cup dried tomatoes, diced

1 tsp. garlic, minced

1 tsp. red pepper flakes

salt

Directions:

1. Combine all ingredients in the stainless steel insert.

2. Seal the lid and adjust the steam release handle.

3. Press MANUAL and cook on HIGH for 20 minutes.

4. Release the steam naturally.

Holiday Whole Chicken

(Prep + Cook Time: 25 minutes / Servings: 4)

Nutritional Info per Serving:

Calories 300, Protein 26, Carbs 0.1, Fat 17

Ingredients:

2 cups water

1 whole chicken

2 carrots, chopped

1 onion, chopped

3 celery stalks, chopped

½ head of garlic, chopped

Herbs, by choice

Salt and black pepper, to taste

Directions:

1. Add the veggies in your Instant Pot.
2. Pour the water into the pot.
3. Top with your chicken.
4. Season with salt and pepper, and sprinkle with the herbs.
5. Close the lid, select MEAT, and cook for 25 minutes.
6. Let sit for 15 minutes before releasing the pressure naturally.

Hot chicken Wings

(Prep + Cook Time: 20 minutes / Servings: 6)

Nutritional Info per Serving:

Calories 600, Protein 88, Carbs 2.3, Fat 24

Ingredients:

½ cup butter

1 tbsp. Worcestershire sauce

4 lb. chicken wings
1 tbsp. sugar

½ cup hot sauce
6 oz. water

Directions:

1. Pour the water into your Instant Pot.
2. Place the wings on the trivet.
3. Close the lid, and cook on MANUAL for 5 minutes on HIGH.
4. Meanwhile, whisk together the remaining ingredients.
5. Release the pressure quickly.
6. Brush the mixture over the wings.
7. Set the Instant Pot to SAUTÉ.
8. Cook the wings for a few minutes, until sticky.
9. Serve and enjoy!

Piña Colada Chicken

(Prep + Cook Time: 35 minutes / Servings: 4)

Nutritional Info per Serving:

Calories 530, Protein 68, Carbs 9, Fat 2

Ingredients:

½ cup coconut cream
1 cup pineapple chunks
tsp. cinnamon

2 tbsp. coconut aminos
2 lb. chicken thighs
½ cup chopped green onion

Directions:

1. Place everything, except the green onions, into your Instant Pot.
2. Close the lid, select POULTRY, and cook for 15 minutes.
3. Release the pressure quickly.
4. Serve topped with green onions.
5. Enjoy!

Butternut Stuffed Turkey Breasts

(Prep + Cook Time: 25 minutes / Servings: 4)

Nutritional Info per Serving:

Calories 447, Protein 38, Carbs 56, Fat 5.5

Ingredients:

2 bacon slices, diced
2 cups white rice
2 turkey breasts
1 tsp. chopped rosemary

1 cup cranberries
1 ½ cups diced butternut squash
3 ½ cups chicken broth
½ cup white wine

Directions:

1. Slice the turkey breasts lengthwise, but not all the way through, to open them like a butterfly.
2. Set your Instant Pot to SAUTÉ.
3. Add bacon, and cook until crispy.
4. Combine rosemary, squash, and cranberries, in the pot.
5. Sauté until the squash is golden.
6. Spoon the mixture on top of the turkey breasts.
7. Roll the turkey breasts, and secure with kitchen twine.
8. Spray some cooking spray into the Instant Pot.
9. Place the stuffed turkey rolls inside, and cook about 3 minutes per side.
10. Transfer to a plate.
11. Add rice and wine, and cook for a few minutes.
12. Pour in the broth and add turkey on top, and close the lid.
13. Select RICE, and cook at the default setting.
14. Release the pressure naturally.
15. Serve and enjoy!

Jam Glazed Turkey

(Prep + Cook Time: 60 minutes / Servings: 6)

Nutritional Info per Serving:

Calories 880, Protein 100, Carbs 80, Fat 20

Ingredients:

1 whole small turkey	½ tsp. cumin
1 carrot, peeled diced	½ tsp. turmeric
5 oz. apricot jam	½ tsp. coriander
1 ¼ cups chicken stock	1 onion, diced
1 tsp. salt	1 ¼ cups chicken stock

Directions:

1. Combine the jam and spices in a bowl. Rub the jam glaze over the turkey.
2. Pour the broth into the Instant Pot, and add the veggies.
3. Add the turkey.
4. Close the lid, select POULTRY, and cook for 30 minutes.
5. Release the pressure naturally.

Chrismas Casserole

(Prep + Cook Time: 45 minutes / Servings: 4)

Nutritional Info per Serving:

Calories 650, Protein 45, Carbs 60, Fat 20

Ingredients:

2 cans of cream of mushroom soup, 10.5 oz.	cubes
	1 bag frozen mixed veggies
1 celery stalk, chopped	4 turkey breasts
1 onion, chopped	1 cup chicken broth
1 bag of Pepperidge Farms stuffing	

Directions:

1. Place all of the ingredients into the Instant Pot.
2. Mix to combine, and close the lid.
3. Select MANUAL, and cook on HIGH for 25 minutes.
4. Release the pressure naturally.

Holiday Duck in Orange Sauce

(Prep + Cook Time: 75 minutes / Servings: 4)

Nutritional Info per Serving:

Calories 447, Protein 50, Carbs 6.1, Fat 22.8

Ingredients:

2 tbsp. fish sauce

2 duck breasts, halved

2 duck legs, halved

9 scallions, chopped

2 red chilies, chopped

2 cloves garlic, minced

1 whole star anise

½ tbsp. diced lemongrass

3 tbsp. chopped ginger

2 cups orange juice

Directions:

1. Set your Instant Pot to SAUTÉ.
2. Add the duck with the skin-side down first, and cook until the skin is crispy.
3. Transfer to a plate.
4. Add garlic, and cook for 1 minute.
5. Whisk together the remaining ingredients.
6. Return the duck to the pan.
7. Cook on MANUAL on HIGH for 30 minutes.
8. Release the pressure naturally.

Roasted Chicken with Thyme and Hazelnuts

(Prep + Cook Time: 55 minutes / Servings: 6-8)

Nutritional Info per Serving:

Calories 446, Protein 43.1, Carbs 55.3, Fat 4.8

Ingredients:

4 lb. whole chicken
¼ cup oil
3 tsp. fresh thyme, minced
3 tsp. lemon zest
1 tbsp. garlic powder
¼ tbsp. red pepper flakes

3 cups chicken broth
3 cups wine, divided
4 tbsp. butter
1 cup cranberries
1 tbsp. sugar

Directions:

1. Brush the chicken with oil. Melt butter in the stainless steel insert of the Instant Pot and press SAUTÉ.

2. Place the chicken inside and sprinkle with thyme, lemon zest, flakes and garlic power. Brown it for 3 - 4 minutes.

3. Pour in 2 cups of wine and the chicken broth. Close the lid and set the steam release handle. Press MANUAL and cook on HIGH pressure for 25 minutes.

4. Release the pressure naturally and remove the chicken from the pot; set aside.

5. In a small pot, add the remaining wine, cranberries, sugar, and 1 cup of broth from the Instant Pot.

6. Bring to a boil, and then cook for 12 - 15 minutes, until the cranberries are completely soft.

7. Put the sauce into the chicken's cavity.

8. Serve warm or cool.

Roast Leg of Lamb

(Prep + Cook Time: 60 minutes / Servings: 6-8)

Nutritional Info per Serving:

Calories 389, Protein 41.3, Carbs 15.7, Fat 17.1

Ingredients:

2 lb. lamb leg, rinsed and drained
1 lb. potatoes, whole
1 tsp. garlic powder
⅓ cup red wine vinegar

1 lemon, sliced
3 tbsp. oil
1 tbsp. fresh rosemary, chopped
1 tsp. brown sugar

Directions:

1. Place the lamb and the potatoes in your Instant Pot, and cover with water.
2. Season with salt and garlic.
3. Close the lid, set the steam release handle and select MEAT function.
4. When you hear the off signal, perform a quick release and open the lid.
5. Remove the meat and the potatoes. Take out the liquid and keep it.
6. Rub the meat with oil and rosemary.
7. Return it back to the Instant Pot.
8. Pour in wine vinegar, sugar and add lemon.
9. Add 1 cup of the reserved liquid and close the lid.
10. Press MANUAL and cook for 7 minutes.
11. Perform a quick steam release.

Roast Goose

(Prep + Cook Time: 40 minutes / Servings: 8-10)

Nutritional Info per Serving:

Calories 521, Protein 40.3, Carbs 2.8, Fat 36.1

Ingredients:

2 lb. goose fillets, cut into 1-inch thick slices
1 cup onions, chopped
4 tbsp. butter, softened
2 garlic cloves, crushed
3 tsp. fresh celery, chopped
1 ¼ cups white wine
2 bay leaves
1 tbsp. dried thyme
¼ tsp. white pepper, ground

Directions:

1. Season the meat with salt and white pepper.
2. Place it at the bottom of the Instant Pot and add bay leaves, thyme, wine and 2 cups of water.
3. Close the lid, set the steam release handle and hit the MEAT button.
4. Perform a quick release and remove the everything from the pot.
5. Melt butter, on SAUTÉ function.
6. Add onion and garlic, and stir-fry for 4 minutes.
7. Add goose fillets and brown each one at the time for 3 minutes.
8. Serve and enjoy.

Beef Fillet with Prosciutto and Horseradish

(Prep + Cook Time: 45 minutes / Servings: 8)

Nutritional Info per Serving:

Calories 426, Protein 51.8, Carbs 5.5, Fat 18.3

Ingredients:

2 lb. beef fillet, center cut
6 oz. prosciutto
3 cups beef stock
1 onion, chopped
2 tbsp. butter
1 cup red wine
⅓ cup horseradish sauce
1 tsp. thyme, dried

Directions:

1. Rub with thyme. Melt butter in the Instant Pot and press SAUTÉ.
2. Add the onion and stir-fry for 3 minutes.
3. Add the fillets and brown them on both sides, one fillet at the time.
4. Place back all browned fillets into the pot and add in the red wine and the beef stock. Close and select MANUAL for 30 minutes.
5. Perform a quick release and remove the fillets, placing them on a serving platter.
6. In a saucepan, combine the horseradish sauce and the prosciutto. Stir-fry it and drizzle over the fillets.

Apple Cider Partridge

(Prep + Cook Time: 55 minutes / Servings: 4)

Nutritional Info per Serving:

Calories 433, Protein 41.4, Carbs 28.1, Fat 20.4

Ingredients:

2 partridges, cleaned and prepared
1 cup onion, chopped
2 Alkmene apples, cut into pieces
1 cup apple cider
2 cups chicken stock
¼ cup celery stalks, chopped
¼ cup olive oil

Directions:

1. Grease the Instant Pot with olive oil and select SAUTÉ.
2. Add the onion and stir-fry for 3 minutes.
3. Add celery and apples. Cook for 6 more minutes, stirring occasionally.
4. Add the meat, apple cider and chicken stock.
5. Seal the lid and set the steam release handle.
6. Press MANUAL and cook for 35 minutes. Perform a quick release and serve.

Roast Turkey with Spices

(Prep + Cook Time: 60 minutes / Servings: 6)

Nutritional Info per Serving:

Calories 473, Protein 29.4, Carbs 13.4, Fat 12.1

Ingredients:

2 lb. boneless turkey breasts, halved
2 garlic cloves, crushed
3 cups chicken broth
2 cloves

½ cup soy sauce
1 tsp. basil, dried
1 tbsp. cane sugar
¼ cup oil

Directions:

1. Place the meat in a zipper bag and add cloves, basil, soy sauce, oil, and 1 cup chicken broth. Seal the bag, shake and refrigerate for 35 minutes.
2. Grease the Instant Pot with oil and add garlic. Stir-fry for 3 minutes.
3. Place the turkey in the pot along with 3 tbsp. of the marinade and the remaining cups of chicken broth.
4. Seal the lid and set the steam release handle. Cook on MANUAL for 25 minutes. Allow for a natural pressure release.

Honey and Mustard Glazed Duck

(Prep + Cook Time: 45 minutes / Servings: 4)

Nutritional Info per Serving:

Calories 463, Protein 32.3, Carbs 75.1, Fat 10.1

Ingredients:

1 lb. duck breast
3 cups chicken broth
1 cup honey
¼ cup soy sauce

¼ cup dry sherry
1 tsp. oil
1 tsp. Dijon mustard

Directions:

1. Place the meat in your Instant Pot and add the chicken broth.
2. Seal and press MEAT.
3. When done, perform a quick release and remove the meat and the broth.
4. Select SAUTÉ and grease the stainless steel insert with oil.
5. Add soy sauce, honey, sherry and mustard. Stir well and cook for 5 minutes.
6. Add the duck and coat well.
7. Serve immediately and enjoy.

Slow Cooked Beef Sirloin with Wine

(Prep + Cook Time: 12 hours / Servings: 4)

Nutritional Info per Serving:

Calories 461, Protein 51.9, Carbs 12.3, Fat 17.1

Ingredients:

2 lb. beef sirloin
3 cups beef consommé

1 cup red wine
1 bay leaves

Directions:

1. Add in all ingredients. Seal the lid and set the steam release handle.
2. Set to SLOW COOKER mode and set the timer to 11 hours.
3. When done, release the pressure naturally.

Christmas Poussin with Bacon

(Prep + Cook Time: 50 minutes / Servings: 4)

Nutritional Info per Serving:

Calories 413, Protein 31.5, Carbs 8.3, Fat 33.4

Ingredients:

1 young chicken
6 oz. bacon
2 cups chicken stock

2 tbsp. butter
½ cup Worcestershire sauce

Directions:

1. Place in the meat, chicken stock and Worcestershire sauce.
2. Close and set the steam release handle.
3. Press MANUAL and cook for 45 minutes.
4. In a skillet, melt the butter and add the bacon. Stir-fry for 2 minutes.
5. Perform a natural release and remove the chicken from the pot.
6. Serve with the stir-fried bacon.

Slow Cooked Braised Venison

(Prep + Cook Time: 11 hours / Servings: 4)

Nutritional Info per Serving:

Calories 392, Protein 47, Carbs 10.3, Fat 9.5

Ingredients:

2 lb. leg of venison
2 garlic cloves, whole
3 cups beef stock
1 cup red wine
1 onion, chopped

2 tbsp. butter, softened
2 celery, chopped
1 tsp. fresh thyme
1 bay leaf

Directions:

1. Place all ingredients into your Instant Pot and select SLOW COOKER mode.
2. Set the steam release handle and adjust to 11 hours.
3. When done, perform a natural pressure release.
4. Transfer to a deep pot and cook until half of the liquid evaporates.

Swedish Meatballs

(Prep + Cook Time: 20 minutes / Servings: 4)

Nutritional Info per Serving:

Calories 740, Protein 42, Carbs 50, Fat 42

Ingredients:

2 cans of cream of mushroom soup, 10.5 oz.

16 oz. egg noodles

1 cup sour cream

1 ½ cups beef broth

24 oz. cooked and frozen Swedish meatballs

1 cup milk

Directions:

1. Combine all of the ingredients in your Instant Pot.

2. Close the lid, select MANUAL, and cook on HIGH for 11 minutes.

3. Release the pressure naturally.

Herbed Meatloaf

(Prep + Cook Time: 55 minutes / Servings: 4)

Nutritional Info per Serving:

Calories 263, Protein 9, Carbs 2, Fat 14

Ingredients:

2 lb. ground beef

1 tsp. thyme

1 tsp. rosemary

1 tsp. oregano

1 tsp. parsley

1 tsp. garlic powder

2 eggs

3 tbsp. olive oil

Directions:

1. Pour 2 cups of water into your Instant Pot.

2. Grease a loaf pan with the oil.

3. In a bowl, combine all of the remaining ingredients.
4. Press the mixture into the loaf pan.
5. Place in the Instant Pot, and close the lid.
6. Select MANUAL, and cook on HIGH for 30 minutes.
7. Release the pressure quickly.

Holiday Beef Roast

(Prep + Cook Time: 50 minutes / Servings: 4)

Nutritional Info per Serving:

Calories 499, Protein 50, Carbs 30, Fat 16

Ingredients:

2 tbsp. olive oil
2 tbsp. Italian seasonings
2 lb. beef roast
4 potatoes, cubed
4 carrots, peeled and chopped

3 celery stalks, chopped
1 cup beef broth
1 cup red wine
2 tbsp. steak sauce

Directions:

1. Set to SAUTÉ. Heat the olive oil, and brown the meat on all sides.
2. Place the remaining ingredients into the pot.
3. Close the lid, select MANUAL, and cook on HIGH for 35 minutes.
4. Release the pressure naturally.

Smokey Cranberry Pulled Pork

(Prep + Cook Time: 55 minutes / Servings: 10)

Nutritional Info per Serving:

Calories 525, Protein 36, Carbs 40, Fat 26

Ingredients:

2 cups cranberries

¼ cup buffalo wing sauce

½ cup apple cider vinegar

1 cup tomato puree

½ cup water

1 tbsp. adobo sauce

1 chipotle pepper, diced

2 tbsp. tomato paste

⅓ cups molasses

3 tbsp. liquid smoke

Directions:

1. Combine the water and cranberries in the Instant Pot on SAUTÉ, and cook for 4 minutes. Stir in the remaining ingredients.

2. Close the lid, and select MANUAL. Cook on HIGH for 40 minutes.

3. Shred the pork with a fork, in the Instant Pot. Stir to combine.

Applesauce Pork Chops

(Prep + Cook Time: 40 minutes / Servings: 4)

Nutritional Info per Serving:

Calories 420, Protein 38, Carbs 20, Fat 20

Ingredients:

2 tbsp. flour

1 tsp. cinnamon

½ cup brown sugar

1 ½ lb. pork chops

4 apples, sliced

1 tbsp. olive oil

Directions:

1. Set the Instant Pot to SAUTÉ.

2. Heat the olive oil, and cook the pork until browned. Set aside.

3. Add half cup of water, and scrape the Instant Pot's bottom.

4. Stir in the remaining ingredients, and return the pork to the pot.

5. Close the lid, and select MANUAL. Cook on HIGH for 10 minutes.

6. Release the pressure naturally.

Glazed Ham

(Prep + Cook Time: 35 minutes / Servings: 6)

Nutritional Info per Serving:

Calories 630, Protein 42, Carbs 60, Fat 20

Ingredients:

1 tsp. ground cloves
1 cup brown sugar
½ cup honey

4 tbsp. crushed pineapple
1 ½ cup water
5 lb. ham, boneless

Directions:

1. Make slits in the ham. Add the water to your Instant Pot.
2. Sprinkle the ham with sugar, and brush with honey.
3. Sprinkle with the cloves, and top with the pineapple.
4. Close the lid, and select MANUAL. Cook for 20 minutes on HIGH.
5. Release the pressure naturally.

Ham and Peas Side

(Prep + Cook Time: 50 minutes / Servings: 6)

Nutritional Info per Serving:

Calories 185, Protein 13, Carbs 10, Fat 5

Ingredients:

5 oz. diced ham
1 lb. peas

6 ½ cups stock

Directions:

1. Place all of the ingredients into your Instant Pot. Close the lid, and select MANUAL. Cook on HIGH for 30 minutes.

2. Release the pressure naturally, for 10 - 15 minutes.

Bean Nachos

(Prep + Cook Time: 35 minutes / Servings: 6)

Nutritional Info per Serving:

Calories 263, Protein 17, Carbs 45, Fat 11

Ingredients:

2 cups dried pinto beans
1 onion, quartered
½ cup cilantro salsa
1 tsp. cumin
½ tsp. black pepper

1 tsp. chili powder
3 cups veggie broth
1 tsp. paprika
4 garlic cloves, chopped
1 tsp. salt

Directions:

1. Place all of the ingredients in your Instant Pot. Stir to combine.
2. Close lid, select MANUAL, and cook on HIGH for 28 minutes.
3. Release the pressure naturally for 10 minutes.
4. Blend the mixture with a hand blender.

Bean and Tomato Dip

(Prep + Cook Time: 15 minutes / Servings: 4)

Nutritional Info per Serving:

Calories 40, Protein 1, Carbs 5, Fat 1.5

Ingredients:

½ can cannellini beans
1 tsp. minced garlic
3 sun-dried tomatoes

½ onion, chopped
1 tsp. paprika
1 ½ tbsp. oil

½ cup water

½ tsp. salt

1 tsp. lemon juice

½ tbsp. capers

Directions:

1. Set your Instant Pot to SAUTÉ.
2. Heat the oil, and cook the onions and garlic for 4 minutes.
3. Stir in paprika and salt, and cook for 30 more seconds.
4. Place the remaining ingredients, except lemon juice and capers, into the pot.
5. Close the lid, select MANUAL, and cook for 15 minutes.
6. Stir in the lemon juice and capers.
7. Blend the mixture with a hand blender.

Holiday Brussels Sprouts with Bacon and Goat Cheese

(Prep + Cook Time: 35 minutes / Servings: 6)

Nutritional Info per Serving:

Calories 140, Protein 10, Carbs 8, Fat 8

Ingredients:

2 tbsp. water

6 cups Brussels sprouts

¼ tsp. salt

¼ cup crumbled goat cheese

5 bacon slices, chopped

2 tbsp. balsamic reduction

Directions:

1. Set the Instant Pot to SAUTÉ.
2. Add bacon, and cook until crispy.
3. Add Brussels sprouts, salt, water, and balsamic reduction.
4. Cook for 6 minutes, stirring occasionally.
5. Serve topped with goat cheese.

Buttery Lobster

(Prep + Cook Time: 25 minutes / Servings: 4)

Nutritional Info per Serving:

Calories 190, Protein 19, Carbs 0, Fat 12

Ingredients:

4 lobster tails

¼ cup butter, melted

½ cup white wine

1 cup water

Directions:

1. Cut the tails in half. Pour the water and wine into your Instant Pot.

2. Place the lobster in the steaming basket.

3. Close the lid, and select MANUAL. Cook on LOW for 4 minutes.

4. Release the pressure naturally. Drizzle with melted butter.

Cumin and Bean Dip

(Prep + Cook Time: 25 minutes / Servings: 4)

Nutritional Info per Serving:

Calories 500, Protein 18, Carbs 50, Fat 23

Ingredients:

1 ½ cups great northern beans, soaked overnight, drained

6 tbsp. lemon juice

2 garlic cloves, minced

1 tbsp. cumin

1 ½ tbsp. chili powder

3 tbsp. minced cilantro

Salt and black pepper, to taste

Directions:

1. Drain the beans and place them in the Instant Pot.

2. Cover with about 1 inch of water.

3. Close the lid, select MANUAL, and cook on HIGH for 13 minutes.
4. Allow pressure to release naturally.
5. Drain and transfer the beans to your food processor.
6. Add the remaining ingredients. Pulse until smooth.

Pressure Cooked Hummus

(Prep + Cook Time: 35 minutes / Servings: 6)

Nutritional Info per Serving:

Calories 109, Protein 13, Carbs 15, Fat 4

Ingredients:

6 cups water
¼ tsp. cumin
1 cup chickpeas, soaked overnight, drained

3 garlic cloves, crushed
2 tbsp. tahini
¼ cup chopped parsley, for garnish
Juice from 1 lemon

Directions:

1. Place chickpeas, water, salt, and garlic in your Instant Pot.
2. Stir to combine.
3. Close the lid, select MANUAL, and cook on HIGH for 18 minutes.
4. Allow pressure to release naturally.
5. Place the chickpeas in your food processor, but save the cooking liquid.
6. Add lemon juice, cumin, tahini, and ½ cup of the cooking liquid to the food processor.
7. Process and add more of the cooking liquid, as needed, until the hummus reaches your desired consistency.
8. Serve and enjoy!

Party Oysters

(Prep + Cook Time: 15 minutes / Servings: 6)

Nutritional Info per Serving:

Calories 142, Protein 7, Carbs 1, Fat 12

Ingredients:

6 tbsp. melted butter

36 oysters, cleaned

Directions:

1. Place the oysters in the Instant Pot along with the 1 cup of water.
2. Close the lid, and select MANUAL. Cook on HIGH for 3 minutes.
3. Release the pressure naturally. Serve drizzled with melted butter.

Scalloped Potatoes

(Prep + Cook Time: 15 minutes / Servings: 6)

Nutritional Info per Serving:

Calories 168, Protein 4, Carbs 30, Fat 3

Ingredients:

2 tbsp. potato starch
1 tbsp. chopped chives
1 cup chicken broth
6 potatoes, peeled and sliced

1 tsp. salt
⅓ cup milk
⅓ cup sour cream
1 cup chicken broth

Directions:

1. Combine the potatoes, broth, salt, and chives in the Instant Pot.
2. Close the lid, select MANUAL, and cook on HIGH for 5 minutes.
3. Release the pressure quickly. Transfer the potatoes to a plate.
4. Whisk the remaining ingredients into the Instant Pot.

5. Cook for 2 minutes. Return the potatoes to the pot. Cook for 2 minutes.

Thanksgiving Maple Carrots

(Prep + Cook Time: 10 minutes / Servings: 6)

Nutritional Info per Serving:

Calories 80, Protein 1, Carbs 16, Fat 1.5

Ingredients:

2 lb. carrots, peeled   1 tbsp. butter, melted
¼ cup raisins   1 tbsp. maple syrup

Directions:

1. Combine half cup of water, carrots, and raisins in the Instant Pot.
2. Close the lid, and select MANUAL. Cook on LOW for 4 minutes.
3. Release the pressure quickly. Whisk together the maple and butter.
4. Brush the glaze over the carrots.

Carrots in Bacon Blankets

(Prep + Cook Time: 25 minutes / Servings: 6)

Nutritional Info per Serving:

Calories 144, Protein 4, Carbs 8, Fat 11

Ingredients:

1 lb. carrots, peeled   1 tsp. white pepper
1 tsp. paprika   ¼ cup chicken stock
1 tbsp. olive oil   ¼ tsp. marjoram
9 oz. bacon, sliced

Directions:

1. Combine the herbs and spices in a small bowl. Sprinkle over the carrots.
2. Wrap each carrot in a bacon slice.
3. Heat the oil in the Instant Pot.
4. Add carrots, and SAUTÉ for 10 minutes.
5. Pour the broth.
6. Close the lid, select MANUAL, and cook for 2 minutes on HIGH.
7. Release the pressure quickly.
8. Serve and enjoy!

Boiled Peanuts

(Prep + Cook Time: 80 minutes / Servings: 4)

Nutritional Info per Serving:

Calories 200, Protein 15, Carbs 16, Fat 20

Ingredients:

2 tsp. Cajun seasoning   ¼ cum sea salt
1 lb. raw peanuts

Directions:

1. Clean the peanuts by removing twigs or roots.
2. Place them in the Instant Pot.
3. Add sea salt, and cover with water.
4. Close the lid, and select MANUAL.
5. Cook on HIGH for 70 minutes.
6. Release the pressure naturally.
7. Sprinkle with Cajun seasoning.
8. Serve and enjoy!

Stewed Pears in Red Wine Sauce

(Prep + Cook Time: 15 minutes / Servings: 6)

Nutritional Info per Serving:

Calories 232, Protein 1, Carbs 37, Fat 1

Ingredients:

1 bottle red wine
2 cups sugar
6 pears, peeled
1 bay leaf

1 1-inch ginger piece
1 cinnamon stick
4 cloves

Directions:

1. Pour the wine into your Instant Pot.
2. Stir in the bay leaf, cinnamon stick, sugar, ginger, and cloves.
3. Add the pears.
4. Close the lid, and select MANUAL.
5. Cook on HIGH for 5 minutes.
6. Release the pressure naturally.

Fancy Stuffed Peaches

(Prep + Cook Time: 35 minutes / Servings: 6)

Nutritional Info per Serving:

Calories 143, Protein 1.5, Carbs 25, Fat 2

Ingredients:

6 peaches, pits removed
1 ½ cups water
½ tsp. almond extract, divided
2 tbsp. butter

½ tsp. cinnamon
¼ cup cassava flour
¼ cup maple syrup

Directions:

1. Combine half of the almond extract and the water, in your Instant Pot.
2. Combine the remaining ingredients in a bowl.
3. Divide the mixture between the peaches.
4. Place the peaches in the steaming basket.
5. Close the lid, and select MANUAL.
6. Cook on HIGH for 3 minutes.
7. Release the pressure quickly.

Chocolate Almond Candy

(Prep + Cook Time: 30 minutes / Servings: 6)

Nutritional Info per Serving:

Calories 122, Protein 3, Carbs 16, Fat 6

Ingredients:

14 oz. condensed milk
2 cups water
1 tsp. milk

1 cup chopped almonds
12 oz. chocolate chips
1 tsp. vanilla

Directions:

1. Pour the water into the Instant Pot.
2. In a heatproof dish, add chocolate chips and condensed milk.
3. Cover with foil, and place in pot.
4. Close the lid, and select MANUAL.
5. Cook on HIGH for 3 minutes.
6. Stir in the almonds and vanilla.
7. Line a baking sheet with parchment paper.
8. Drop teaspoons of the mixture onto the paper.
9. Freeze until set.

Conclusion

Now that your recipe folder is richer by 365 irresistible Instant Pot delicacies, the next step is to get your money's worth for this revolutionary appliance. I dare you to try all of these delights!

Did you like these recipes? Leave a review and share your cooking experience. Your feedback is deeply appreciated!

Thank you and happy cooking under pressure!

DEAR READER

Thank you so much for purchasing this book. I've put a lot of hard work into making this a great resource for both experienced and beginner cooks and I hope you get an immense amount of value out of the book.

I know that not everyone likes to write book reviews but would you mind taking a minute to write a review on Amazon? Even a short review works and it would mean a lot to me and it will help me to improve and to provide a better quality product.

If someone you care about is struggling with anxiety or workaholism, please send him or her a copy of this book.

Finally, if you'd like to get free bonus materials from this book and receive updates on my future books, you can sign up for my newsletter at:

http://sixweeksweightloss.com/

Life awaits. Go #Instant Pot!